7 CARD STUD

42 LESSONS

D0391632

About the Author
Roy West is the best-known poker teacher in Las Vegas. His popular column, "This and That About Poker," regularly appears in *Card Player* magazine. West has played poker professionally for many years in the card barns of Southern California and casinos of Las Vegas.

Dedication
This section is the toughest of all to write. So many people—so much help—not only with this Course, but with life. I've decided to dedicate this book to someone who knows nothing about poker, yet—Cody, my six-year-old best buddy who never stops asking questions, and who has taught me everything I know about ghost busting and ridding the neighborhood of monsters. May he grow up to be all his mom wants him to be (and a hell of a poker player, like I taught his mother, Cindy, to be).

The
Complete
Course in
Winning!

7 CARD STUD

42 LESSONS
How to Win at Medium & Lower Limits

Roy West
Cardoza Publishing

FREE EMAIL NEWSLETTERS
AVERY CARDOZA'S NEW EMAIL GAMBLING NEWSLETTERS:

Avery Cardoza's Poker Newsletter
Avery Cardoza's Gambling Newsletter
Avery Cardoza's Online Gaming Newsletter

When you sign up for Avery Cardoza's newsletters, you receive three newsletters for free: Avery Cardoza's Poker Newsletter, Avery Cardoza's Gambling Newsletter and Avery Cardoza's Online Gaming Newsletter. Our newsletters are packed with strategy tips, free money sign-up bonuses to online sites, pre-publication discounts, tournament information, and words of wisdom from the world's top experts, authorities, and World Champions.

SIGN UP NOW—IT'S FREE!!!

www.cardozapub.com

FIRST CARDOZA EDITION

Copyright © 1996, 2004 by Roy West

- All Rights Reserved -

Library of Congress Catalog Card No: 2003113845
ISBN: 1-58042-137-7

Visit our web site (www.cardozapub.com) or write
us for a full list of books and advanced strategies.

CARDOZA PUBLISHING
P.O. Box 1500, Cooper Station, New York, NY 10276
Phone (800)577-WINS
email: cardozapub@aol.com
www.cardozapub.com

COURSE OF STUDY

PART 9
TOURNAMENT TACTICS

PART 10
CAN I MAKE A LIVING PLAYING LOW

Foreword

BY JUNE FIELD
1982 Ladies Seven-Card Stud
World Champion of Poker

The game of poker is like life—the amount of effort you put into it determines the rewards you'll receive from it. To succeed in life takes knowledge, experience, determination, and hard work. Yes, you'll make mistakes and meet with failures along the way, but these too serve a purpose. *These same attributes apply to poker.* Add healthy doses of patience, self-discipline, and a positive attitude and you'll have what it takes to be a winner in life and at poker.

But wait, there's one key element that you'll need to add to complete your recipe for success and that's *skill*, or what Roy West refers to as the "stuff."

I've seen Roy's stuff in practice at both ring games and in tournaments. He's simply awesome! And his rare talent for teaching others—through both his private poker lessons and through his solid advice in his regular poker column—speaks highly for him as a person who can communicate in a way that is easily understood.

Roy has *finally* made his poker expertise, knowledge, and strategies on seven-card stud available to the poker world through his *Seven-Card*

Stud: The Complete Course in Winning at Medium and Lower Limits. In it, he takes you through every step of the game, introduces you to the proper strategies for your three-card starting hand through seventh street, and teaches you everything you need to know to become a winning stud player.

Roy's Rules apply to the game's psychological maneuvers and thought processes—his "Play Happy" rule leads the pack! I strongly suggest that you study Roy's book as faithfully as a preacher studies his bible, and you'll be on the road to becoming a strong stud player. I studied Roy's "stuff" for two years and it helped me win the women's world championship in 1982. *Enough said?*
♠

Acknowledgments

This is the place where the author (that's me) thanks the people who came through when needed, thereby saving his butt in some instances. The order of mention was determined by drawing the names out of a brandy snifter.

Dana Smith edited my jumble of words into readable form and suggested some additions that I hadn't thought about. She then prodded, poked, cajoled, and nagged me until I actually went to my word processor and came back with the material. What a pain she turned out to be.

Because of Tom McEvoy, this is the only seven-card stud book that has a chapter on seven-card stud tournament tactics. The 1983 World Champion of Poker has thereby made this Course that much more valuable to you.

June Field created the finest poker and gambling publication in the world, *Card Player*, and allowed me a voice in it as a regular columnist. She was no stranger to poker before that, having won the ladies world championship of poker in 1982. Valuing her opinion, I asked June to do the foreword to this Course. As I write these acknowledgments, she is probably in her office writing the foreword, so I won't see it until the Course is printed. I hope she said something nice.

I've learned more about poker from Mike Caro than anyone should be allowed to learn. Gives me too much of an edge. I suppose that's why, a few years ago, I dubbed Mike, "The Father of Modern Day Poker." (Several other noted poker authorities were a bit ticked at me about that one.)

If I were being politically correct, Linda Johnson should have been mentioned first, being my "boss," so to speak. And she gives the best hug in the Las Vegas valley. ♠

Introduction

I wish a Course such as this had been publicly available when I first began playing seven-card stud. The information was available, but only to a select few. The professionals had it, but they weren't telling. The few books available were primer level and incomplete. And no one was giving poker instruction. I would gladly have paid a ton of bucks for the information and strategy lessons printed here, *and I would have considered it a bargain!*

For years my students have been asking me to put my Course Lessons into print. It was they who told me about the gaps in the books, even now, years later. They complained that the books in print were either for the lowest of limits and didn't go into enough detail, or were for higher-limit players. There was nothing for the medium limits they wanted to play.

I decided to fill that gap with my Course, and include the latest low-limit information, to enable low-limit players to learn the strategies necessary to win consistently and to move up to even bigger wins at the medium limits.

This is the first major seven-card stud book in over six years. It contains the very same information that many players paid $520 for in my private one-on-one lessons. Now it is available to you.

I have organized and presented this information as though you are a student sitting across the table from me having a discussion about how to win at seven-card stud medium and lower limits. It's like having your favorite uncle, who is a professional poker player, teach you how to win at poker.

Roy West

The "Stuff" of Winning Poker

Introduction

Winning consistently at poker takes skill and knowledge—what we call strategy. But it takes more than that.

COURSE LESSON 1

IT TAKES THE RIGHT "STUFF" TO WIN AT POKER

From this Course, you'll learn what I call the "stuff" of winning poker. Trust me. In my private one-on-one lessons, I've taught hundreds of players to win consistently over the years in Las Vegas and Reno, in California and Atlantic City, and points between. These students who have proven to be the most consistent winners are the ones who built a solid foundation on what I'll refer to in this text as poker *stuff*.

It is the stuff of poker that will make you a consistent winner. *Stuff* means anything important to winning that isn't strategy. And some of the most important points we'll look at in this Course deal with *stuff*.

This Course gives you the winning strategy of Las Vegas professionals at the limits of $1-$4, $5-$10, and $10-$20. Plus the winning stuff!

Anyone can pick up on the strategy. Yet many have studied on their own and still aren't winners. No one has told them about the stuff of winning poker. Lucky you! You're about to learn it. ♠

COURSE LESSON 2

POKER IS A PEOPLE GAME

Poker is not a game of cards. It is a game of people. We only use cards and chips to keep track of what's going on. In fact, poker is the only game in the casino where your decisions, pitted against your opponent's decisions have a direct influence upon your winning or losing. It is the only game you don't play against the house. You play poker against other players: *people*. Therefore...

There is no substitute for knowledge of your opponents!

Make a big note filled with those words. Tape it to your bathroom mirror where you'll see it every day. Write it in blazing letters on the insides of your eyelids. Learn it until you have assimilated it as part of your being.

Your success at the game of poker will depend in large part on how much you take this fact to heart—and then how well you develop that knowledge.

You have to know as much about them as you possibly can so you know how to play against them. Study your opponents—how they play.

What will they raise with on third street? What will they call a raise with? What will they limp in with?

Learning to play poker—strategy and rules and such—is relatively simple. More difficult is getting inside your opponent's mind.

What *is* his frame of mind? It might change tomorrow or in an hour. What gets him on tilt? Does he have a strategy? What is it? Does he deviate from it, consciously or by tilt? And how far?

How do his starting requirements differ from yours? This is extremely important, as you'll see from this example:

I was playing in a newly-started $10-$20 seven-card stud game in which I was familiar with all the players except one. This man sat two seats to my left, which meant that he almost always acted after I did. I began to study his play.

What I quickly learned was that he raised on third street every two or three hands. What I *needed* to know, and also know quickly, was whether he was just getting a hot run of good hands, or if his starting requirements differed from mine.

My problem was that I couldn't enter a pot with a hand such as a low or medium pair because I couldn't stand the raise that was almost sure to come.

My study of him intensified. I paid particular attention to his cards whenever he showed them at the end of a hand. It wasn't long before I discovered that he was raising at third street with every three-straight or three-flush he held—never with any pairs. I don't know where he learned this strategy, but it must still be costing him dearly. I say "still" because it cost him that night, from his stack to mine.

Now, with specific knowledge about this opponent, I was able to play him to my advantage. Now I could enter the pot with a hand like a pair of eights. If he raised, fine. I reraised and got it heads up with him while I was holding the better hand. Thus, I was able to clean his clock.

There is no substitute for knowledge of your opponents!

Is he gambling? Or is he all tucked in, waiting for the nuts before he'll invest in the pot?

Notice and remember everything about him and the *way* he plays. And *why* he plays. For fun or for money? Much of what you will learn from this course is based upon this important principle.

When you know how an opponent tends to play, it's easier to put him on a hand because there are fewer possibilities to consider. You should study a new player right from the first moment you see him, even if you are at the rail waiting for a seat. In fact, that's a good place to begin gathering knowledge of your opponents.

Rather than walking around shooting the breeze, just killing time, get on the rail and watch the game you will be playing in. Study the players you haven't seen before. When you're on the rail for twenty minutes, you can gather much information about a player, and *he has none about you* when you sit in his game. It's an easy way to get an edge on your competition.

Never stop studying your opponent. Not today. Not next week. Not next year. You can never know too much about him. What is the texture of the hands you see him play? Is he a check-raiser? A slow-player? Will he raise with a drawing hand? Some players rarely bluff. Some raise on a whim. Some are super-solid, selectively aggressive, well-disciplined, consistent winners (my students). You need to know "who is which is what." So you need to "get a book" on each of your opponents.

Most players who keep a book on their opponents keep that book in their heads. But just to let you know what you are up against—the seriousness of many of your potential opponents—I'll tell you that many poker players, both pro and semipro, keep an actual, written book on their opponents.

When one of these serious players encounters a new opponent at the table, he immediately starts a book on him. He'll chat with the newcomer, learn his name and where he's from, *and closely observe how he plays.* Periodically he'll walk away from the table and write notes about the new player in a small notebook he carries just for that purpose. When he goes home he transfers this information into a small spiral notebook which he always takes with him whenever he goes to play.

Later, when he finds himself in a game with a player he might have played against some months before during the tourist's long weekend stay in town, the "book writer" goes out to his car, looks up Mr. Tourist ("Jim from Toledo"), and finds the information on how Jim plays. If you play seven-card stud at the medium limits in Las Vegas, you are in one or two of these books.

And by the way, in any public poker room you might play in anywhere across the country, you are going to be competing against my students. So you'd better get all of this down cold. *They have.* ♠

COURSE LESSON 3

REMEMBERING EXPOSED CARDS: IT'S EASIER THAN YOU THINK

When I first came to Las Vegas many years ago and began to play seven-card stud seriously, I was bothered by the fact that there were so many cards to remember. Several times I took working players aside and asked them about this problem. The answer I kept getting was, "I have the same problem. Let me know if you figure it out."

So I set about figuring it out. I figured and contemplated and pondered. While pondering (or was it during contemplating?), the answer flashed quietly into my mind. *We make it much tougher than we have to.* It looks like a big job remembering all of those cards laying out there. But actually, that's not necessary.

Let's say that four people fold on third street and four stay to play. You also stay. You won't need to remember *your* exposed card because there it is, right in front of you. That leaves three other players in the hand. And you won't have to remember *their* cards either, because they are laying right out there in front of them.

So now we can see that the problem is *smaller* than it looks. No point remembering a card that is still in plain sight. So on third street, we have to remember only the four cards that have been folded. Put them into memory as they fold. Let's say that they are folded in this order: nine, jack, seven, four. Rearrange them in your mind as four, seven, nine, jack. You'll find it easier to remember them in sequence. (I prefer starting with the lowest card and going to the highest because that's the way I learned to count—up. Some players prefer it the other way around. Take your choice.)

It will be a rarity that you'll have to, or be able to, see and account for all thirteen of a suit. Take note if you've seen more than three of a suit. That will make it unlikely that an opponent is drawing to a flush in that suit. If you see two or fewer of a suit, consider that suit to be live.

At fourth street, suppose that two other players fold, two cards each. Put them into memory in sequence as they fold. Now a total of eight cards have been shown and folded. *And that's all you have to remember.* Eight cards. There are now only two players left in the hand, you and one opponent, and all upcards will now stay on the table until either one of you folds or until there is a showdown.

With different numbers of players folding at different streets, these numbers will change. But for the most part, you will be required to memorize only nine or ten cards at the most. And that's a lot easier than trying to remember every card shown during the entire hand. Simple, huh? You're welcome. ♠

COURSE LESSON 4

READING HANDS

Reading your opponents' hands is both an art and a science. It is a hard-to-learn skill that combines logic and intuition, and even after you have learned how to do it, you then need experience to make it work. *Lots* of experience. And of course, that I can't give you.

As you gain experience, your logical thought processes will come together more quickly. With some mileage under your belt, you'll also be better able to make more accurate guesses (intuition) about your opponents' hands. Your guesses, your intuitive calls are, I believe, nothing more than your subconscious collecting information and feeding it to your conscious mind as strong feelings. Some players call this process "getting a feel for the game." Pay attention to them but don't rely on them until your experience tells you they are trustworthy. Meanwhile, stay mostly with logic.

The main ingredient you'll need in reading hands is knowledge of your opponents.

Such reading is difficult, if not impossible, without that knowledge. The two are intertwined. Different opponents play differently in the same situation. You need to know how your current opponent plays the situation. *See Course Lesson 2.*

It is easier to read good players because they tend to be in the pot with stronger hands (hands of specific value) than weak players who could be in with almost anything. Therefore, realize that it will be easier to read your opponents at the $5-$10 and $10-$20 medium limits than at the low limits such as $1-$4. That's why it is easier to beat the medium limits than the low limits—another good reason to develop your poker skills and move up.

The best time to study your opponents is when you are out of a hand and not financially or emotionally involved. Never mind the game on TV or trimming your toenails. Stay alert to the poker game and observe all. *Study* your opponents while they are playing—and while they are *not* playing. Then you'll have a basis for comparison when you think you've spotted a tell. For example, you might notice a player begins taking short, quick puffs on his cigarette during a hand. You might assume that he has just made a good hand. But what you didn't notice is that he also periodically takes several short, quick puffs when he is out of a hand.

The best time to get a read on what hands and cards your opponent will start with at third street is after the hand is over—at seventh street, the showdown. Here you will have an opportunity to see his entire hand.

When he gets his last, facedown card, watch to see where he places it among his other two downcards. If it goes on top of the other two cards and it stays there, his two starting cards will be on the top when he turns over the three cards at the showdown. Easy. If he places it on the bottom and it stays there, the opposite is true. If he places it in the middle, between the other two downcards, and it stays there, the two outside cards will have been among his starting cards. If he shuffles the three together, you can't use this method, but you *can* tell, logically.

For a simple example, if your opponent has raised on third street showing a four, you can logically figure that he *didn't* raise with a split pair of fours. But you want to know what he *did* raise with. At the showdown, he turns over two queens and a six. You can logically assume that he started with two queens in the hole with his four upcard, and not a queen and a six in the hole with his four up.

If a player makes a flush with exactly five of his seven cards, and if three of his suit are turned over at the showdown, you know that he is willing to stay and pay to the end with a drawing hand.

When you're doing this seventh street read, don't look at the first hand being turned over like everyone else will be doing.

Instead, *listen* while you concentrate on the hand not yet shown. The dealer will announce the first hand turned over. Listen for that, as you watch the other player's hand. If he sees that he is beaten, he will most likely throw away his hand without showing it. But he might inadvertently flash the hand, or show it quickly to a neighbor, and you may get a glimpse. Then you can turn your eyes to the winning hand, which will still be laying there.

When a new player sits down in your game, you'll also want to get all of the information about him that you can, as quickly as you can. Begin observing immediately. What does he do with his chips after he buys in? A player who puts his chips in a sloppy pile, sort of stacked and sort of not stacked, is usually a loose player with no organization, no plan, just playing.

The player who stacks his chips very neatly, even lining up the colors on the edges, is more likely to be a conservative player. He probably has a plan for playing, rather than playing randomly or on a whim. He is an organized person and probably plays in an organized way with some kind of strategy. It will be easier to determine his strategy than that of the player who has no plan. After all, if *he* doesn't know what he's doing, how are *you* going to figure it out?

Notice also *when* he does the neat-stacking of his chips. He'll do it while he is out of a hand, of course. But that means that while he is busy stacking his chips into pretty piles, he isn't observing the other players. In that regard he's the same as the player who watches the ball game on.

Something I love to see is an opponent who is playing half a dozen Keno tickets, has wagers on a couple of horses, and is watching two games on TV on which he also has bets. What he's *not* doing is playing poker.

7 CARD STUD

Here are a few quick tips on reading hands:

• A player pairing his *fourth* street card is more likely to have two pair than trips.

• A player who makes a flush is most likely to make it in the suit of his doorcard.

• A player cannot have a full house at fifth or sixth streets without showing at least one pair. The same is true of four of a kind at fifth and sixth. But be aware that at seventh street, it is possible for an opponent to have a full house, or even four of a kind, *with no pair showing on his board.*

• For a player to have a straight flush on seventh street, he must be showing at least two of its cards on his board—at fifth and sixth streets, at least three.

Suppose that after getting his seventh-street card, a player looks at his three downcards, and then at his upcards, and then at his downcards, and then at his upcards. Why? He's trying to figure out if he has made a straight. Even a novice can see a flush at a glance. But for many players, a straight has to be figured out and put in order.

Here's another interesting read that not many players know about: A player bets on the end and doesn't get called. If he takes another look at his hand, kind of a quick-peek before tossing it in, he has made something big. He looks again because his hand is "pretty." He wants to see it one more time before giving it up—it is probably a flush. He wouldn't be as likely to take a last peek at a straight because a straight is not as pretty as a flush or a full house.

A betting pattern to watch for in spread-limit games, where players can choose the size of their wagers, is known as The Milk Route. Most players who use it do so regularly, almost as a habit, without thinking about it. In a $1-$5 game, a *milk route* player bets $2 at fourth street. At fifth street his bet is $3. His sixth-street bet is $4. Seventh street brings the maximum $5 bet. Milk-route bets are made in comparable amounts in bigger spread-limit games such as $2-$10.

This player has what he believes to be a big hand and wants to milk it to keep you in the pot. He wants you to be thinking, "It's only $2. I'll look at another card." Then, "It's only $1 more than the last bet. What the heck—I'll take off another card." And so on. If your opponent had a marginal hand, he either wouldn't bet at all, or he would bet the maximum to get you out. He doesn't, so he wants you in.

A $1 or $2 bet doesn't always mean that your opponent is on the milk route. But otherwise, what does each bet size mean? That's what you have to determine from observing and remembering. The meaning of a bet will be different in different opponents. A $1 or $2 bet might mean that he is just timid, not much of a gambler, and wants to bet—but not "a lot." Many players will make a small bet at fourth street when they have a four flush. Their logic is that they want to get some money into the pot in case they make the flush, but don't want to bet much in case they miss. Only thorough observation will get you this kind of knowledge of your opponents.

An opponent's maximum bet might mean that he wants you out of the pot because he has a medium-value hand that he would like to win with right now without taking any further risk. Or it could mean that he has strength enough to beat you, but he believes that you have enough of a hand to call his maximum bet.

Players who raise at third street at the low and medium limits almost always have what they are representing, which is usually a big pair.

Most players want to limp in if they have a three-straight or three-flush so as to get the proper odds to draw to the hand. Or if they don't understand those odds, they just want to play the starting hand as cheaply as possible until it turns into a complete hand. Some will raise with big cards in their straight or flush starts, so a raise from an ace doesn't always mean a pair of aces. Study your players so that you'll know what they tend to do.

Some players never raise with a drawing hand, so a raise from them showing an ace or a king usually means that they have a pair of that card or a hidden medium pair. It could also mean big trips. That's a long shot, but that doesn't mean it couldn't happen. If you put an opponent on a big pair when he really has trips, it will probably cost you some money. That's why they call it gambling. But most players won't raise at third street with big trips.

If an opponent raises at third street showing a high card, two out of three times expect him to have a split pair of that rank. If someone raises at third street showing a small card, you'll want to know if he has a pair of that card, or a larger hidden pair. The smaller his upcard, the less likely he is to be raising with that pair. Figure him for the large buried pair, or if he is a player who raises with three-flushes, give him two big cards in the hole of the same suit as his upcard.

With some players, a raise with an ace showing at third street is actually more likely to be a pair of aces if there is another ace showing elsewhere on the board. With one of his aces gone, the raiser feels even more compelled to protect his pair of aces because the chances of improvement are diminished. This same player will often be the type to *not* raise with aces if he figures they are all live, giving him a better chance of improving. This concept also applies to the other big pairs. Now it's up to you to figure out which players do what.

If an opponent who has just limped in at third street is raised, and then he reraises, suspect a powerful hand, no matter what he is showing. He most likely has a big pair at the least, higher than any upcard showing, and quite probably three of a kind.

Again, reading hands is largely an art. It is difficult to formulate a lot of rules for reading hands, so I am showing you some examples that will give you the flavor of the reading process—some guidelines to help you in most situations. Now let me give you a few more examples and reading concepts before wrapping this up.

Some players don't walk the way they talk.

Many players use table talk to mislead you. For example: It's checked around to a player and he says, "We have to get some money in this pot so I'll start the contributions." He has a hand he thinks will be a winner.

Or suppose that on a later street, a player makes a maximum bet, firing his money into the pot while saying, "Call that if you don't like money." Would he say that if he had a powerhouse he knew would beat you? Certainly not. This fits in with the central theme of Mike Caro's *The Body Language of Poker*: Most players try to act weak when they are strong, and strong when they are weak.

A player bets at seventh street without looking at his last card. He's trying to give you the impression with his blind bet that he is already so strong that the last card doesn't matter. If that were true, would he want to announce it to you, cutting off your call? Certainly not. He'd be trying to look weak so that you would call his bet. Instead he's trying to look strong so that you *won't* call his bet. He's probably on a flush or straight draw, is hoping you won't call, and hoping that he made it if you do call. Most of the time, he didn't make it, so if there's any money in the pot, call.

If a player just limps in showing the ♥10 with three or four more hearts showing on the board, unless he is a complete dolt, you can assume that he isn't starting with three hearts. It is more likely that he has a pair or a three-straight. Trips are a possibility, but are a long shot. If two other tens are showing on the board, he most likely has a small or medium pair in the hole. He probably wouldn't be playing with a dead pair of tens.

Say your opponent's upcards at fifth street are 5-8-6, all offsuit, in that order. He called a bet at fourth street, and now when he gets the six at fifth street, he raises. Most players will give him credit for a straight. But wait—think back to third street. Would he have started with a 4-7 in the hole and a five showing? Maybe, if they were suited. But then he got an unsuited eight at fourth street and still played. He probably wouldn't call a bet holding only an 8-to-1 shot three-straight in four cards. He probably has two pair or trips. By the way, most novice to intermediate players will give you credit for the highest hand you could possibly be holding, and then play you that way.

Let's say that an opponent calls your third-street raise showing a small heart. At fourth street he gets another small heart. You bet. He raises. At fifth street he catches a club. You check, and instead of the bet that you expect, he checks along behind you. He probably has a flush draw. His fourth-street raise was intended to buy a free card on fifth street, which it did. If he catches a heart on sixth street, play him for a flush.

The following thoughts are for women. You men can skip past this, or read it for your own protection.

Ladies, if you don't get to see a male player's hand at the showdown, *try asking him what it was.* That's right: Just ask him. Ask him in a nonchalant, friendly, mostly-just-curious way, what he had. You'll be surprised how many men will answer you.

Being a female player, you have an advantage in learning how your male opponents play. Male players seated around you will be more willing to show you their hands, or let you peek at their cards when you're out of a hand. This allows you to get a line on their play. Because there are many more men than women playing public poker, you will probably have a man seated on each side of you. Take advantage of both of them. Sounds like dirty pool, doesn't it? But if you're playing to get the money, take every edge you can get.

Many men (the predominant gender in public poker rooms) don't expect you to be a good player—probably just a novice at public poker who has played only in home games on the kitchen table. You'll have a surprise for them when you have mastered this Course. They will underestimate you. Good! Play solid poker and take the money.

Be friendly at the poker table. Talk a bit, joke a bit, but lightly. Keep the mood jovial and you won't be considered as a threat in the poker game. Then your male opponents won't be upset when you beat them out of a pot. They'll think you just got lucky.

Much of this advice will also be of value to a young male player, who will also tend to be underestimated as a threat by the older guys at the table. Generally, most of the men in public poker rooms will be approaching middle age or older, and have been playing poker for several or even many years. Pretend you are a novice who got lucky.

And now a final warning that applies to us all. At third street, you want to put a player on several possible hands. Then, as the hand progresses, you can eliminate some of them on the succeeding streets, always thinking back to see if his previous actions fit your current assessment. My warning is this: It's a mistake to put a player on *one* specific hand, and then not be willing to change your assessment if his play warrants it.

This is as much as I have to say on reading hands. I suggest that you study this Lesson in tandem with *Lesson 2, Poker Is A People Game*. There is no substitute for knowledge of your opponents when it comes to reading hands. ♠

COURSE LESSON 5

Solid Poker Gets the Money at These Limits

One more important piece of *stuff* before we get to the strategy of seven-card stud: Remove from your mind the idea that the consistent winners at low and medium-limit poker are the players with the smooth moves and sophisticated strategies. It ain't necessarily so. Solid poker is what gets the money at these limits—and the consistent winners are the players *who make the fewest mistakes.*

It doesn't matter how good you can play: What matters is how good you do play!

Play solid poker as mistake-free as possible and you will be a consistent winner. ♠

Third Street Strategy

Introduction

All right, before you blow a gasket, let's get to the winning strategy—what to do when you are actually sitting at the table with your money on the line.

This is the moment. A stir of excitement as you enter the fray. An adrenaline rush. "Can I remember everything I've learned from Roy's Course?" Yes, you can. So let's get to learning it.

All strong, solid players agree:
Your most important decision
in seven-card stud is whether to play
after seeing your first three cards.

7 CARD STUD

If you start weak, you'll probably end up weak. If you start strong, your hand is that much stronger when it improves. The idea is to either start strong or with a hand that can become strong with the next card. A potential problem that is created when you improve a weak hand is that you will probably not become as strong as a player who started with a strong hand.

Also, when you do improve your weak starting hand, you may find yourself feeling committed to it for another round or two. This can become very expensive. As I am so fond of saying, "Your first mistake is the costly one." If you don't make the first mistake for a dollar or two on third street, you *can't* make a couple of $20 mistakes later in the hand. And third street is your first opportunity to make a mistake.

Before we can proceed, you'll need to know the difference between fixed-limit and spread-limit games. Most casino poker games with limits of $3-$6 and up are fixed-limit games. You can bet or raise only a fixed amount, the lower of the two limits, up to fifth street. At fifth street and beyond, you can bet or raise only the amount of the upper limit of that game.

In spread-limit casino games, which are common at the $1-to-$5 level, you may bet any amount between the lower and upper limits at any time. In a $1-$5 game, you can bet or raise $1, $2, $3, $4, or $5. In a $2-to-$10 spread-limit game, you can bet or raise any amount between $2 and $10 at any time.

COURSE LESSON 6

THIRD STREET TRIPS

Let's look at starting hands for seven-card stud. We'll begin with the hand you're least likely to be dealt: trips. The odds are 424-to-1 against your getting *any* three-of-a-kind for your first three cards, so they won't show up very often... once in about every ten hours of play.

The nature of starting with trips is:
They will either win you a stack,
or lose a stack or two.

When you start with any three-of-a-kind, the odds are good for making a full house: about 2-to-1. You also stand a good chance of winning without improvement. Now the question is whether to raise with these trips here on third street, or to just limp in with them. The answer: It depends. At the low and medium limits which we are studying, your trips should be played slow if they're big, fast if they're small.

If your trips are tens or higher, just call any bets. Now this next sentence is almost always a surprise to my students, and they often start disagreeing with me before I can make my explanation. With three nines down through three deuces, *raise!* While these are strong hands, they are vulnerable—not only to straights and flushes, but also to higher trips. If you start with, let's say, three fours and an opponent starts with a pair of sevens and then catches another seven, he has you locked up—especially if his starting sevens are hidden. So raise. Narrow the field. Protect your trips. Get that pair of sevens out on third street.

My students have often asked, "But isn't a big set such as three kings also vulnerable to straights and flushes?" Yes, but a big set is not vulnerable to three sevens. You have a lot more wins slow playing big trips and taking your chances against straights and flushes. If you start with three kings, you'd love to have a player in with a pair of sevens and hope he makes three of them.

Out of the three things that can happen, two are good for you. If you both fill, you win. If you both miss, you win. If your opponent fills but you don't—bummer. Now add this:

When you hold any three-of-a-kind and the pot is raised ahead of you, tend to reraise. In spread-limit games, make it the maximum.

Ideally, you will now play this hand against the raiser and possibly one other player. But this is not an automatic raise. Let's say you're in late position holding three fives here at third street. A jack raises and a king reraises. Do you put in another raise?

It depends on whether you want to announce the strength of your hand or lay in the weeds. When you reraise in that circumstance (showing a five), you are saying that you have either a hidden pair of aces or three fives. If I had seen one or two jacks or kings in the upcards of players who have folded, I would tend to raise to get more money in the pot, hoping the jack and king would both stay with me.

But if I haven't seen any jacks or kings, their hands would be live and my three fives would be more vulnerable, so I would tend to *not* raise. My raise would be an attempt to knock out the jacks. It might, but the kings would stay. The player with the jacks (if he values his bankroll) would probably drop anyway just because of the reraise from the kings.

Another major consideration is the type of game you are playing in—tight or loose.

In a tight game, tend to raise less with trips at third street. In loose games, tend more toward raising in close decisions.

Generally, the smaller your trips, the more you'll tend to raise for protection. As an aside and for your general information, playing at the higher limits, you would tend to raise with the big trips at third street because raising would look more natural. For example, players in the big games tend to raise showing an ace, whether or not they have another one in the hole. And of course, they almost always raise with two aces. So if you know a player will raise with one ace or with two aces, but does not raise showing an ace, what could he have? Of course—three aces. So not raising in the big limits showing an ace doesn't look natural, and therefore arouses suspicion. File this information away for when you move up to play $50-$100.

When I recommend a third-street raise in a spread-limit game, I'm talking about a bet that is three-quarters the allowable maximum (for example, a raise of $3 in a $1-to-$5 game), unless your experience with your opponents indicates that a maximum bet is needed to narrow the field sufficiently.

A bonus you get with your third-street raise is this: Anyone who calls your raise probably has a stronger than average starting hand—and so it will be easier for you to judge what that hand is. ♠

COURSE LESSON 7

THIRD STREET
A HIGH PAIR, 10S OR BETTER

I see a big problem in the play of many low and medium-limit poker players—a little knowledge is a dangerous thing. They see other players raising with big pairs on third street so they say, "I'll do that, too." And they do it every time. And they don't even know why they're doing it.

**With a high third-street pair,
you will usually want to raise—
usually, but not always.**

Many players holding a high pair on third street always limp in (just call), hoping to keep other players in. Incorrect! The more players drawing against your high pair, the higher the chances of your being outdrawn.

**Your big pair is a favorite against a
single straight or flush draw. Against
several such draws, you are still a
favorite against each of them
individually—but collectively,
you become an underdog.**

So your third street raise with a big pair is for protection. You want to narrow the field and, ideally, play against one opponent with a smaller pair or a drawing hand. You wouldn't be bad off if you had one of each.

A note of caution. Before you go charging into a pot raising your hot big pair with chips splattering the table, stop and look—especially if you have 10s or jacks. You're looking to your left for players with overcards. (To the right, too, but more on that later).

If you're about to raise with a pair of jacks, especially if they are split (one is down and the other is your upcard), check first to see how many overcards there are behind you (to your left) yet to act. If there are two or more, I suggest just limping in. If one of the overcards raises, you can call if your jacks are hidden (both of them are in your downcards) and *live* (no other jacks are showing on the table), and if your kicker is higher than the raiser's doorcard (his first upcard).

With only one overcard behind you, go ahead and raise.

If you are reraised by an overcard, again you can call *only* if your jacks are hidden and live, and your kicker is bigger than the raiser's probable pair. The idea here is to avoid playing your pair straight-up against a bigger pair. But I like to take off a card if *all* my cards are live *and* my kicker is an overcard to his announced pair.

Playing a smaller pair against a bigger pair makes me an underdog. So why do it? I will only do it if my pair is hidden. If my pair is split, no—no play. What's the difference? If my pair is split, my opponent will see the improvement when I catch the third jack and can easily read my hand. Less profit for me. But if the pair is face down, my power is hidden when I catch the third jack. Calling the raise costs the same in each instance, but the implication at the start is that I will make more money with the hidden hand.

I talked earlier about looking to your left for overcards before raising at third street. Here's a caution for low-limit players, $1-$5 and under. *Check to the right also.* Be aware of any overcards that have *not* raised. In these medium and lower-limit games, players often are not aware that they should be protecting their big pairs.

The fact that an ace or a king just limped in does not mean that he doesn't have a pair of that rank.

In the big games, players will often limp in with a big pair as a means of setting a trap. In the small games, they often just limp in with no particular strategy in mind (such as a trap). But the results can be the same. So don't trap yourself into discounting the possibility that a player to your right holds a big pair just because he didn't raise on third street.

COURSE LESSON 8

THIRD STREET
MIDDLE PAIRS, 7s, 8s, 9s

My thinking here is to be conservative with middle pairs at the start in medium and lower-limit stud games. At the big limits, you'll often see players ram and jam with these middle pairs, especially if their kicker is an overcard to the board. But at our limits, your *primary* concern is the quality of your kicker—not deciding whether you will raise, but whether you will *play.*

Automatically raising with middle pairs at these limits will cost you a lot of money in the long run.

So let the big kids splash around. That's fine for them because their games are more aggressive, due largely to what is known as an overante, compared to our limits. That means that their ante is a larger percentage of the bet size. For example, at $10-$20, as the game is dealt in Las Vegas, the ante is $1. At $20-$40, the ante is $3. Notice that the limits have increased by 100 percent, but the ante has gone up 300 percent. And as the limits increase, the ante size increases by a greater percentage each time. This encourages aggressiveness. But at our limits, with a smaller percentage ante, being conservative works better.

ROY WEST · CARDOZA PUBLISHING

You'll want to consider several things in deciding whether to play a middle pair on third street. What is the quality of your kicker—how high is it? What is your position? Are you in the "steal" position (last to act with only the low card and perhaps one other caller in the pot)? *See Lesson 15 on ante stealing.* Are your cards live? Is your pair hidden or split? What are the other players' doorcards (first upcards)? Let's look into these questions, and hopefully come up with some workable answers.

First, your kicker. How big is *big*? Standard poker wisdom says that if you start with a small or medium pair, your sidecard (another word for *kicker*) should be an ace. That's because an ace would be an overcard to the board and would give you a shot at the highest two-pair if you pair your kicker. I modify that to say that your kicker should be an overcard to the *board*, but probably not lower than a queen or jack. After all, when you play these middle pairs, your objective is to hit three-of-a-kind or a *big* two-pair at fourth street. If your kicker is a small one, then you *can't* make a big two-pair. Worse yet, if you pair your small kicker on fourth street, you have trouble (more on *trouble* as we get farther along).

Let's suppose the dealer blesses you with a split pair of sevens and an ace kicker—you have a seven showing with an ace and another seven in the hole. Your cards are all live. The low card tosses in the bring-in money. Do you play? Yes. Live cards and an overcard kicker: yes. But what if there is a raise before the action gets to you—do you play? I do if I can see that there will also be one other caller (and hopefully, he will be on a draw). However...

In an instance like this, look for reasons to not play.

Does it look as though there might be another raise behind me? I'm gone, thank you. I have found a reason *not to play.* If my kicker with those two sevens is a jack instead of an ace, I don't call the raise. At these limits, it is most likely that the raise will come from a pair higher than jacks. And if the raise comes from *exactly* a jack, then my jack kicker is a dead doornail.

As I attempt to put the raiser on a hand, I'll want to see if his cards are live here on third street. So I'm saying that I'll stand one raise with a medium pair and a definite overcard kicker. But if I have to call a double raise, I'll fold my tent, *even if* my kicker is that magic ace.

Now let's say that you have called with a split pair of nines in early position. A conservative player raises showing a small upcard. You know that this player raises *only* with large pairs, so he has something big buried. In this instance, your smaller pair has a legitimate call against a bigger pair. This is contrary to some of what we have already discussed. "What's up?" you ask. What's up is that it now becomes easy to read your opponent's hand. He cannot make two pair without your seeing it, except on the last card. If he pairs his doorcard or any other card before seventh street, you can see the pair laying there and will know that he has two-pair, and you can play accordingly.

We've talked about being willing to call a raise with a *hidden* pair, especially if your kicker/upcard is higher than the pair you figure your opponent raised with. But if there are still players to act after you who have higher doorcards than the upcard of the raiser, especially if they are aggressive players, you should fold because you are in danger of a reraise behind you. You can stand one raise in this situation, but not two.

Generally, when you hold a medium or small pair on third street with one of your pair-cards showing on the board, you should pass—unless your kicker is an overcard to the board and is no smaller than a queen.

That overcard gives you the possibility of making the highest two-pair, in addition to improving your pair to trips if you catch the last available card of your rank. But the biggest factor in determining whether to play a pair with one of your cards already out is your position in relation to where that card is on the board.

Let's say that I have a pair of eights. If my needed eight is in front of me (must act before I act) and plays, I'm gone. The fact that he played indicates a strong possibility that he has the last eight in the hole, especially if my two eights are hidden—because then he can't know that his eights are dead. If he folds, I can figure that he doesn't have another eight and so I can play—assuming that I have a big overcard.

However, if my needed eight is to my left and must act after I do, I don't know if he's going to play or not. I don't have enough information to make a correct decision, so I'll take a brief moment to glance to my left to see if I can pick up a clue as to his intentions. Often, you can see a player reaching for his chips long before the action gets to him. Or you can tell that he is ready to toss his hand when it's his turn to act. If he indicates that he intends to fold, I play. If he is reaching for his chips, I fold. And if I can't tell either way, I have to fold because of my lack of information.

I hope you've noticed the stress put on high kickers in determining whether many of your hands are playable.

Seven-card stud is a game of live cards.
It is also a game of high kickers.

Here's another example. Suppose you put your opponent on a pair of jacks while you hold a medium or even a small pair. For you to play, you must have an ace, king, or queen *in the hole* for a kicker. You don't want it to be your upcard because you will probably have to act first at fourth street. Since your hand is not strong enough to bet, you'll have to check, showing weakness. A savvy opponent will jump all over that, betting strong on every card. Unless you get immediate, significant improvement, you'll be in a position of checking and calling, which is indeed a weak, meek (and generally losing) way to play poker. So, as a general summary:

**Middle pairs should be played
conservatively at these limits,
with a lot of consideration given to
big cards as kickers.**

Tend to not call raises unless you have a specific, profitable looking situation. If there has been no raise, limp in cheaply (just call). You're looking to make exactly three of a kind at fourth street, or two high pair if your kicker is a high one. And, by golly, I hope you've gotten it tattooed on your brain by now: big kickers, big kickers, big kickers. ♠

COURSE LESSON 9

THIRD STREET
SMALL PAIRS, 2s THROUGH 6s

Generally speaking, these small pairs are played much the same as the middle pairs except that, of course, they are more vulnerable. You'll have to be more alert to when you think that you are beat. And, of course, it's more likely that a pair of threes is going to be outrun than a pair of eights.

Of prime importance again is your kicker/ sidecard: *big!* The bigger, the better. I'll repeat: You can't make a big two-pair if you start with a small kicker. Any improvement at fourth street is more likely to be to two-pair than to trips. Assuming that your cards are live, there are three cards you can catch to make two-pair and two cards to make trips.

Small pairs almost always play better if they are hidden, mostly because of the surprise value when you make trips.

Also, with your small pair in the hole, your kicker is your upcard, and it will be big (hopefully, an overcard to the board). This type of hand is among the most difficult for your opponents to read. If you have the biggest upcard and don't raise, they will most likely put you on a drawing hand (a big straight or high flush). When you trip up at fourth street with the same suit as your high doorcard, most opponents at the medium and lower limits will be sure that you are on a flush draw. You'll have a surprise for them later on.

When you pair your doorcard at fourth street, they may misread you again, probably putting you on a three-flush with a big pair.

A small pair with a small kicker is also playable, but not very often. The two instances you might play them are in late position with no danger of a raise—with all your cards absolutely live; and when you think you can ante-steal with them from a late position. ♠

COURSE LESSON 10

THIRD STREET
THREE-TO-A STRAIGHT FLUSH

First, don't get all bent out of shape: You're not going to make a straight flush. Or at least, it's not very likely. After all, how many have you made in your poker-playing life? Okay, okay... it is possible. It'll happen about 1-in-66 times you start with this hand. That's a probability of 1.49 percent.

If you are holding three *big* cards to a straight flush, you can play it a couple of ways. First, if two (or three) of your three high cards are overcards to the board and if they are live, consider raising, especially in late position with three or four players having already limped into the pot. If you drop most of them, you have provided protection for your hand when you pair up on fourth street, and you have also gotten some dead money into the pot (money put in by players no longer active in the hand). If most of them stay with you, you have good pot odds for drawing to a straight or a flush (or even a straight flush) if one of those hands falls to you at fourth street.

With the same situation in *early* position, the purpose of your raise would be to narrow the field in anticipation of making an overpair at fourth street. But if your cards are not really live, you'd be cutting your own throat with a raise because there wouldn't be much of a chance for the overpair, and there probably wouldn't be enough money in the pot to give you the correct money odds for drawing to a straight or a flush. So just limp in.

If your three-to-a straight flush starting hand does not have overcards, it really isn't as strong as you think. You have no chance to make an overpair.

I recommend setting aside the thought of making a straight flush until it happens—then it's a bonus. What you have here at third street are two starting hands: a small three-straight and a small three-flush. That too will get many players overly excited, being able to go for two hands. But maybe they don't have as much as they think.

I don't like either hand very much. I hate small straights—wouldn't touch 'em with a titanium fork. There is no way a *small* straight draw can become a *big* straight. At least a small three-flush can become a big flush by catching two or three high suited cards. I'll call a raise with this hand, but I won't *be* the raiser.

When you start with three-to-a straight flush, your board observation must be very swift because there are so many more exposed cards in other players' hands that are of interest to you—the three ranks that will pair you; the number of your suit that are out; and how many of your straight cards are exposed See *Course Lesson 3, Remembering Exposed Cards*. Busy, busy. ♠

COURSE LESSON 11

THIRD STREET THREE-FLUSHES, QUALITY AND NON-QUALITY

Quality, non-quality—what's the difference? Answer: Overcards. Three big suited cards, overcards, would be the most "quality" of quality flush starts. But a three-flush with just two big cards, overcards, also makes a quality flush start in my book (and this *is* my book, thank you).

At the other end of the scale, a 7-4-2 suited would be the least quality of flush starts. But what you really want to know is how they play, or are played, differently. Then you got here just in time...

How you play a three-flush, whether you play it at all, depends on several factors.

They include how big your cards are (quality or non-quality three-flushes), what you are showing for an upcard, your position, and most importantly, how many of your suit are already out in other players' third-street hands.

Let's eliminate one play right away: If you see that *more* than *two* of your suit are out, toss a non-quality three-flush unless you're in the perfect spot for an ante steal. It's not worth playing with three or more of your suit gone. If you have a quality three-flush, you can afford to have *three* of your suit out. That's because you now have ways to get significant improvement other than extending the flush draw at fourth street by pairing one of your big cards.

If you have seen *none* of your flush cards exposed, almost any three-flush is playable. An exception would be if you have three small cards and someone raises before the action gets to you. Players who raise on third street at these limits almost always have the power they are representing. Almost. It's up to you to determine which players will raise representing, but not holding, power. Again, there is no substitute for knowledge of your opponents.

I'm not too thrilled about playing a small three-flush in very early position, no matter how many of my suit are out, if I see several big cards behind me yet to act—especially if those big cards are in the hands of aggressive players who tend to raise a lot without the power they are representing. Just the fact that the player raised with that big card, even if it's his only one, makes me an underdog with my three small cards. And there's always the possibility of a raise from one of those players who *does* have the big pair he is representing.

One of the last things I want to do in a poker game is to play my small flush draw against a big pair heads-up.

I am an underdog in that spot. Even if I win the hand, which I figure to do only about one-in-five tries in this situation, I won't make enough money with only one player putting in money against me to make up for the other four times I put in my money and lose.

So the problem you face with the small three-flush in very early position is that you don't know how many people will call behind you, much less how many will raise. You lack information. Without information, you're guessing. And if you're guessing, you're gambling. The point of learning these concepts is to take the gamble out of your game.

Now let's suppose you have a non-quality three-flush containing just one big card in middle position with no one yet having called the bring-in bet. You call. The next player, showing a jack, raises. Everyone from there on, including the low card, folds. You now find yourself in the position of playing your drawing hand against what is probably a big pair. You are a decided underdog. Call or fold?

Conventional poker wisdom says that you can call such a raise only if your hand includes an ace. Let's modify that:

You should have at least one overcard to the pair you figure your opponent is raising with.

In this scenario, your opponent most likely holds a pair of jacks. Your one big card is a hidden queen, a *live* queen. Call or fold?

Wait a minute. We haven't considered a raise. If your opponent is an aggressive "Fast Eddie" type, a reraise from you will probably bring another raise from him. And you certainly don't want to get into a raising war against what is probably, but not for certain, the best hand. So just call and take off a card. (Remember: Multi-way, best hand or best draw; heads-up, best hand.)

If that queen, instead of being hidden, is your upcard and if your opponent is a player who is capable of throwing away a pair of jacks (thinking he has been reraised by a bigger pair or by trips that you slow-played the first time around), try the raise. If he calls, you're not in good shape, but you do have outs with your semi-bluff (catching a queen or lengthening the flush). ♠

COURSE LESSON 12

THIRD STREET
THREE-STRAIGHTS,
QUALITY AND NON-QUALITY

In the playing of straights, my biggest concerns are much the same as playing three-flushes: big cards, overcards, live cards, my upcard, and my position.

I recommend only three combinations of straight cards as starting hands—8-9-10, 9-10-J, and 10-J-Q. And the 8-9-10 is marginal. With that starting hand, there is only one possibility of pairing a premium card, the 10, and that's the bottom end of the premium-pairs spectrum. The 9-10-J combination gives you two premium cards to pair, and the 10-J-Q gives you three. And that makes it *much* more powerful than the 8-9-10 start. So, of course, any combinations below that are definitely non-quality. Toss them.

"But," you ask, "what happened to the old 'rule of eight' that says that the smallest straight start should include an eight, so that a 6-7-8 is a playable start?" Well, it's just that: an old rule. Keep playing it if you don't like money.

Then you ask, "What about K-Q-J? Or A-K-Q?" I prefer to put them in the "overcard" category, which I'll go into shortly.

**Big cards give you another way to go
if you don't lengthen the straight:
by pairing a big card. But if you pair,
you'd like the pair to be good.
Thus, the reason for overcards.**

Live cards. How *live?* The "rule of two points" will tell you that. We'll use 9-10-J as an example. Your primary needed cards with this start are eights and queens. The secondary needed cards are sevens and kings. Primary cards that you see on the board are worth one point each; secondary cards are worth a half-point. If you see a total of more than two points, too many of the cards that you need for your straight are dead.

In the above example (9-10-J), if you see an eight and a queen, that's two points. Or two queens would be two points. The same with two eights. Playable. If you see one queen and one seven, that's one and a half points. Playable. Two sevens—one point. Playable. Any combination of two points or under gives you a playable hand from that standpoint. One queen, one eight, and one seven: two and a half points. Not playable as a straight... maybe as an overcard hand. More on this in a moment.

I don't like straights, with the exceptions noted above. I'm not alone in this. I know many professionals who don't play any straights. And a bunch more who will play a few straights, again as noted above, when they have other value.

In a close decision on whether to play or fold, a two-flush gives added value to your three-straight starting hand, assuming the flush cards are *live*. And I want them totally live, because in the direction of making a flush, I have only two for a start. So instead of needing two more suited cards for a flush, I need three.

What about raising with a three-straight? I don't like to do it, mostly because I will be knocking out the very players I need in to get the right pot odds to play the hand. An exception would be as an ante steal.

If no more than one player has limped in while I hold my big three-straight, and if I'm in late position with no higher cards than mine behind me as a threat of a reraise, I'll go for the ante steal (by raising). I'll more than likely drop the low card at these limits. The bigger kids at the higher limits are very likely to play back at you with nothing, knowing that you're on a steal.

If the limper calls, the steal didn't work, but I'm not in too bad a shape. It's unlikely that he's setting a trap for me at these limits. I'd figure his most likely hand to be a medium pair unless I have other specific information about his play to the contrary. There is no substitute for knowledge of your opponents. I still have ways to go because of my predilection for playing only the bigger three-straights.

What about calling a raise with your big three-straight? Depends on what you think you need to beat and what the raiser raised with.

If a player raises early showing a big card, and if you can reasonably put him on that pair, then you'd like to have two overcards to that pair—and they had better be *live.*

Also consider what he raised with. If his raising pair is also one of your big cards, your hand's "liveliness" is much diminished, as far as making one or two pair goes.

If the raise comes from a late position with no one having called the bring-in, and if it looks like an ante steal, try a reraise if you have cards bigger than his doorcard, and if there is no threatening hand behind you. This will work best if your biggest card is your upcard, especially if it is an ace or king. The raiser-stealer can't be sure that you aren't reraising with a legitimate hand, or if you are restealing. If he does decide to call your reraise, it doesn't necessarily mean that he has a legitimate hand. He just might not trust that *you* have a legit hand, but he doesn't want to risk another raise. So he decided to take off a card and see what happens.

Even if he does have a pair, you're not in too bad a shape with your live overcards.

They are *live,* aren't they? I hope so after all this hammering I've done on you about playing live cards.

If you have been the *only* caller and *then* the late position raise comes, try the same reraise as above—*unless* the low-card forced bring-in calls or reraises. He might be suspicious about the late raise being an ante steal, but because you are still in the hand as an unknown quantity, he is more than likely on a legitimate hand. He could have anything—and I do mean *anything,* from trash to trips. I don't want to get caught between these two hands without more power than I now hold.

Against any raiser from any position, you have no call unless you are holding what you can determine to be overcards to his probable raising pair, or his biggest card if he is raising with a drawing hand. An exception would be if you figure him to be on a pure steal. ♠

COURSE LESSON 13

THIRD STREET
ONE-GAP STRAIGHTS

Considering that the focus of this Course in the area of straights is rather narrow, the focus in the area of one-gap straights must also be narrow.

As the term implies, one-gap straights are straight draws that have a card missing from the sequence. With the first of our recommended straights (the 9-10-J), 9-10-Q would be a one-gap straight, since the jack is missing. 9-J-Q would be another, with the 10 missing. In the other recommended straight draw from this Course (the 10-J-Q), 10-J-K or 10-Q-K would be the one-gap straights.

So now the question is, "Do you want to play any of these hands?" Yes, you do, but under the right circumstances. And there aren't many of those circumstances.

We've talked about playing hands with live cards, seven-card stud being a game of live cards.

That continues to hold true, but even more so with one-gap straights. Your "gap" card *must be absolutely live*. And the "rule of two points" which we discussed earlier also applies. If you do fill the gap in your one-gap straight try, you'll want to have live primary and secondary cards available to draw.

You also want at least one overcard—a card in your one-gap hand that is higher than any card showing by a player who is in the pot.

Raising with a one-gap straight usually is done only as an ante steal. Calling a raise requires that you have an overcard to the raiser's probable pair, *and* two suited cards. Those two suited cards will make it considerable easier to make a flush if your hand develops in that direction. And if it does, you'd like to have several players in the pot to build pot odds. However, if your hand develops in the pair area, you'd like to have few players. Play accordingly—passively in the first instance, aggressively in the second.

Having said all this, I'll now add that you won't be giving up much if you decide *not to play one-gap straights.* ♠

COURSE LESSON 14

THIRD STREET
OVERCARDS

If the only value to your hand is in its overcards, you are starting weak but can become strong on fourth street by pairing one of your overcards. But it's usually profitable to play such a hand only in late position at these limits. You'll see why in a moment.

First, some numbers: 3-2 and 2-1. These numbers are an easy method I give my students to remember overcard play. 3-2 means that if you have *three* overcards to the board (three cards higher than any of the other players' upcards), you can call against a maximum of *two* players who have limped in, not counting the low-card forced bet. 2-1 means that if you have *two* overcards to the board, you can call against only *one* player who has limped in, again not counting the low-card. Now we can see why calling with overcards is a late-position play: In early position, we don't yet know how many players will be in the pot.

And did I mention *live* cards? If that's not one of your major concerns in seven-card stud by this time, you are either not paying attention or you are just a hopeless dolt intent upon giving away your vast fortune so that your kids won't get their hands on it.

Is it worth calling a raise with this type of hand? Depends. It always seems to "depend." What hand do you suspect the raiser is holding? If the raise comes from a player with a medium doorcard, and if you know he raises with such hands (you have knowledge about your opponent), you can call with two overcards and even consider reraising with three overcards. The reraise will probably assure you of playing the hand against only the medium pair. That would be best.

What about being the initial raiser? Again, "depends." Will the raise here in late position turn out to be a successful ante steal? That would be good—you'd rather win a small pot than lose a big pot.

Your next best outcome would be to play heads-up against a small or medium pair or, better yet, a drawing hand.

Now what about that K-Q-J and A-K-Q we left dangling in the three-straight Lesson? I put them over here because I'm not too thrilled about playing them as straights. My main interest in them is their overcard value. What I find not so thrilling is catching an ace to my K-Q-J or a jack to my A-K-Q. Then I'd have a straight draw with only one end open—might as well be drawing to an inside straight. Of course, if I catch a ten to K-Q-J, I now have a legitimate straight draw with both ends open, and I'll play it as such.

My main interest is in pairing one of those high cards and continuing on in a hunt for two big pair or a big set of trips. If I back into a straight, that's a bonus, to my way of thinking.

A two-flush among your overcards gives the hand added value, but only if your suit cards are *totally live*. Remember, you are holding only two-fifths of a flush at the start instead of three-fifths, which leaves you a longer road in getting to the flush.

It doesn't seem like hands with only overcard value would be worth playing. But if you play them right, they should win you a couple of extra bets each session.

They are among those hands that offer a good money-making potential often found in low-limit games. When your opponents are not doing much third-street raising, just call a lot in late position when you know that you won't be raised. You can call with many hands that you otherwise might not play, because it's sure to be cheap to get in. Take a shot at getting a perfect card on fourth street. ♠

COURSE LESSON 15

THIRD STREET
ANTE STEALING

I can't let you leave third street before I talk about ante stealing. The low-limit games, in the $1-$4 range, usually don't have an ante. Usually, you won't encounter an ante until you get to about the $3-$6 limit and above. But when you play in a game with an ante, you must think about *ante stealing*.

What is ante stealing and why do you want to do it? (One question at a time please.) First, ante stealing is any time you raise on third street trying to win the antes and low-card bet without opposition, while you do not necessarily hold a hand of value. You are trying to "steal" the antes.

As to why—if done correctly, it can show a profit. If not done at all, if you don't replace the antes you put in on every hand, they will drain you. Figure a $10-$20 game with a one-dollar ante. Figure thirty to forty hands per hour. It's not too difficult then to figure that if you were to just sit and not play a hand, your stack would deplete by $30 to $40 every hour. That's a lot to overcome. You overcome it by ante stealing.

An added benefit of ante stealing is that you will be raising more often at third street, giving you the image of being a fast, aggressive player, while in reality you will be playing "selectively aggressive" poker. There's a Lesson coming up by that title, which will explain the concept.

Now that we know what and why, let's look at how. Ante stealing is almost always done from a late position, after all or most other players have acted. If everyone has folded when the action gets to you, and if there is only the forced-bet low card in the pot, it would be extremely foolish of you to fold and surrender all that money laying out there to what is probably a nothing hand. So you raise. He folds. You profit. So far, so good.

If there are still one or two players to act after you and everyone has folded when the action gets to you, raise if your upcard is higher that either of theirs. If not, fold if you have no value.

If you raise as an ante steal holding a hand of no real value and then someone reraises, *give it up.* Don't be throwing good money after bad. Yes, you'll be bluffed a time or two, but in the long run you will save money.

When another player has already voluntarily entered the pot before the action gets to you, forget about stealing the antes. He came in with something and if you don't also have "something," fold and wait a moment for the next hand.

Steal as many antes as you can as often as you can.

When you eventually get "caught," back off for a while. Remember, when you are stealing antes you are always stealing from the same player to your left. He won't like that and will eventually play back at you with a raise of his own just to put a stop to it. You must do the same thing if and when the player to your right wants to continually steal *your* antes.

Most players will eventually play back at you. But I once had a guy on my left in a $10-$20 game a few years ago that I would like to have there in every game I ever play. He *never* played back at me during a five-hour session. I stole about a dozen antes from him: at $10 a pop—$8 in antes and $2 of low-card money—$120. That's a lot of his antes that I could reinvest in antes of my own.

Every game will be different as to how much ante-stealing you can get away with. It depends on the aggressiveness of your opponents. Pay attention so that you aren't putting your foot into any traps. If they are tight non-callers, steal a lot. If they are loose aggressive types who play back, steal less. But steal you must or watch your stacks deplete a dollar at a time. ♠

COURSE LESSON 16

PLAYING SHORTHANDED

A major point to consider when playing shorthanded (four or fewer total players) is that pairs go up in value while drawing hands go down. That's because in a shorthanded game you almost always will have fewer opponents in each pot than in a full game, so you probably won't be getting the proper odds to draw to straights or flushes. Your knowledgeable opponents will adjust their play more heavily in favor of pairs, just as you should. Don't expect them to be playing drawing hands. The less astute players won't take the short handedness of the game into consideration and will play the same way they do in a full game. Here again, knowledge of your opponents is helpful in determining how you play.

Poker authorities disagree as to whether you should ante steal more often in shorthanded games.

Those who say "more" believe that the much quicker pace of the game will eat up antes at a faster rate. Those who say "less" point out that there is less money to steal because there are fewer antes. You are therefore risking the same size of raise as when the game is full, but for a smaller return.

Under either of these conditions, I want my ante-steal to have a high probability of success. So how often I attempt to steal depends on my opponents—specifically their poker knowledge and their aggressiveness.

Knowledgeable players realize that most opponents will do more ante stealing in a shorthanded game, and so give less credence to a third-street raise as indicating strength. They are more likely to call or even play back at you (reraise).

Aggressive players become even more aggressive and will almost certainly play back at you. I have observed that the dynamic and the psychology of the game changes when shorthanded. I'm not certain why, but my best guess says that it's because shorthanded games almost always have few or no tight/conservative players in them. And what does that leave except loose and aggressive players?

The tight players usually will pick up their chips and leave when they see the game about to become shorthanded. They realize that the game is about to become much faster and much more aggressive. They don't like having to ante at a much faster rate, and they don't like calling all those third street raises that are about to come. So they go. If you stay, be ready for a much faster and more aggressive game. ♠

COURSE LESSON 17

THIRD STREET
REVIEW

Third street is so important that I've devised a special review for it. I want to be sure that you have the specifics, and the concepts, down cold. So let's take a moment during our poker Course to look back at what we've learned so far about seven-card stud strategy on third street. That way I can make sure you're getting all of this. Because if you don't get it, I've wasted my time, and I hate to waste time.

If you hate tests, take this one anyway. Cheating is not only allowed, but recommended, because I want you to get this any way you can.

Here's what will be happening for the next few pages. You'll see the chart representing a poker table. The numbers inside the line of the chart, circled, are the seat numbers, which always start to the left of the dealer and go clockwise around the table, just as in actual play. So the player in the number two seat is at the end of the table to the dealer's left. The player in the number seven seat is at the opposite end of the table from the number two seat. And so forth around the table. This is how table seats are referred to in every public poker game in the country.

You'll notice that next to the circled seat

numbers at the table, I have put a card. This is the third street upcard (the doorcard) for each player. I'll put you into several of the seats, one at a time of course, and tell you the cards you have face down to go with the upcard at that seat. Then come the questions. Ready? Let's do it.

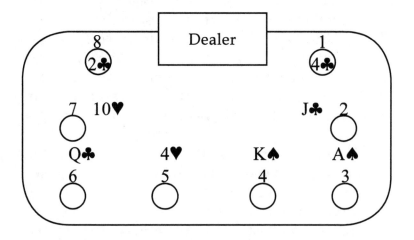

You are in Seat 2. In the hole you have a jack and a seven. The suits are not important for this question, just that you have a pair of split jacks. The 2♣ in Seat 8 opens. The 4♣ in Seat 1 folds. You're next. What to do, what to do.

Yes, a pair of jacks at third street is a raising hand. But wait! Look to your left. There you see an ace, a king, and a queen in the other players' upcards. Too many overcards are yet to act after you. Too much possibility of a reraise that you couldn't call. Just limp in. If those overcards all fold, you'll say, "Hey, I could've raised!" Yes, but the same thing was accomplished anyway, without your risking an additional bet. Be happy.

Remember what we talked about earlier—if there is only one overcard to act after you, put in the raise. Two or more, limp in.

If one of those overcards does raise after you are in the pot, you don't have a call when the action gets back to you. You would if your jacks were hidden, but not when they are split. (Remember the surprise value of *hidden* pairs.)

If you had raised with your jacks and had been reraised by an overcard, you would have no call there either. Some players will continue to play because they have already invested in the pot. Forget that nonsense. Once your chips are in the pot, you have no claim on them unless you win that pot. And there's a fat chance of that happening if you're going to run uphill chasing an overpair.

And besides, your hand is transparent. Your reraising opponent will have little trouble putting you on a pair of jacks, knowing that he has you beat, and will make you pay dearly to try to beat him by betting heavily at every opportunity. Okay, let's move on.

You are in Seat 8. In the hole you have another deuce (your other card doesn't matter). You have a split pair of deuces. After you toss in your forced-bet money, the A♠ in Seat 3 raises. You know from long hours of playing against him that his raise definitely means he has a pair of aces. Do you call? Mercy, no! Your hand not only is *not* hidden, it also is as far from its opponent as it can be in terms of strength.

Now try Seat 4. In the hole you have another king (your other card doesn't matter). You have a split pair of kings. Again the A♠ raises and again you know that he has a pair of aces. Do you call?

Get serious! Certainly not. But in a survey I took a few years ago, many players thought that they should call. First I asked over 200 medium and lower-limit poker players if they would play that same pair of deuces against a known pair of aces. Everyone said, "No way." Then when I asked if they would play that pair of kings against a known pair of aces, sixty percent said they would. When I asked why they would play the kings against the aces when they wouldn't play the deuces against the aces, they said that the kings were much stronger than the deuces. They soon saw the foolishness in it when I pointed out that although the kings were stronger than the deuces, it didn't matter *because kings will always lose to aces.*

Are you getting the idea that you don't want to take any pair against a larger pair? Good. But don't forget the exceptions to this rule: When your pair is hidden, or when your sidecard is higher than your opponent's pair. Having both factors working for you would be even better.

For example, suppose you're still in Seat 4 but now your kings are hidden. The known pair of aces in Seat 3 again raises. Now you have a call because of the surprise value when you make three kings at fourth street. Your opponent with the aces won't know you have three kings and you'll get plenty of action. If you don't make trip kings on fourth street, you haven't invested much. Get out.

When you do make three kings at fourth street (and the player with the aces has not caught another ace), just call when he bets *unless* you perceive that players behind you are drawing to flushes or straights. You want them out. Raise—make them pay a double bet if they want to draw.

When Seat 3 with the unimproved aces bets on fifth street, raise. Get more money in the pot or drive him out. Either way is okay. But if you've seen another or both of his aces fall on the board, reducing or eliminating his chances of making three aces, just call. Give him the chance to make two pair and bet at sixth street. Again, just call. Then raise him on seventh street, or bet if he checks.

Now let's put you in Seat 1. You have 8♣ 9♣ in the hole. Do you play the hand? Why or why not?

If you've been paying attention, you won't play this hand. First, it's a small (non-quality) flush draw in extremely early position. There is too much possibility of a raise from one of those big cards yet to act—a raise you cannot call because you have no overcards. Second, count the clubs showing in the other players' upcards: three clubs. One too many to try for a flush draw with a non-quality start.

Again you are in Seat 1. You have 4♦ 4♥ in the hole. The low card opens. You're next. What do you do?

I hope you said "Raise," because that's what you do to protect this hand of very small trips. Don't let those players with small but higher pairs than yours come in to make a larger set of trips.

If you get a reraise from one of those big cards yet to act after you do, what then? Raise again. You'll get it heads up with the raiser while you are holding the best hand, plus you have driven out the straight and flush draws.

If the reraise comes from the Q♣ in Seat 6, you won't necessarily have tipped the true strength of your hand. There are two pairs higher than his queen with which you could be reraising, as well as with trip fours.

You are in Seat 8. Let's give you another set of trips, but with a different question. You have 2♠ 2♦ in the hole. How do you play? You play the same as with the three fours from the example above—you raise. Yes, you can raise yourself in this situation. If you are the forced low, you can open for the regular low-card bet, *or* for the amount of a raised bet. You are not denied the opportunity to protect a hand just because you are the low card.

Let's keep you in Seat 8 for a moment and give you a pair of aces in the hole. How do you play?

This is the same question you just answered, but with two aces instead of trip deuces. Same answer. When you have any big pair face down while you are also the forced low, bring in the hand with a protection raise—assuming that there is no more than one overcard yet to act after you. If there are two or more overcards yet to act, just limp in.

If you are raised by an overcard, you can still call the raise and take off a card, trying to trip up on fourth-street. Even though your 2♣ is a worthless kicker, you have the advantage of hidden strength. If you don't make trips on fourth street, get out.

Seat 3. Hop over there to the three seat and I'll give you a pair of aces in the hole. Wow, trip aces! After your heart settles a bit, it's your turn to act. The low card in Seat 8 opens. Seat 1 folds and Seat 2 calls with his J♣. What do you do in Seat 3? You just call. Trip aces down through trip 10s, you'll recall (I hope), should be slow-played at these limits. Trip nines down through trip deuces, however, should be protected with a raise.

Seat 6. Now move to the six seat. You'll find Q♦ Q♠ in the pocket. The A♠ in Seat 3 has raised. My, oh my, what do you do now? You reraise, of course! Your reraise announces the strength of your hand (what else could you possibly be raising with?), but that's okay because it will knock all of the drawing hands out of the pot. But your reraise *will* get a call from the aces. A call from the aces? Yes. Kings too, maybe. Jacks, certainly not.

Recreational players at these limits get married to a pair of aces. Those wonderful bullets seem to inspire their holders to believe that another beautiful ace is just waiting to fall into their hands. Dreamers. Gotta love 'em. Gotta. Without dreamers there would be no poker.

Seat 3. You're probably tired of moving all over this table, but do it once more. Put your bottom on the three seat. You have Q♠ 7♠ in the hole. The J♣ in Seat 2 has raised. Your reaction? You can call his raise because you have two overcards (your ace and queen) to his likely raising pair, plus three to a quality flush with only one of your suit showing on the board. You also have one overcard to the king and the queen behind you, in case they enter the pot. You won't get rich playing this hand, but it will show you a long-range profit if you play it conservatively.

That's enough review of third street. I know you're eager to move on to fourth street strategy. Let's move. ♠

Fourth Street Strategy

Introduction

Many players (way too many) have made it a practice (or a habit) to always call at fourth street, because it is usually a small bet in a spread-limit game, and only a half-bet wager in a structured-limit game. Incorrect!

Continue playing because your hand warrants it, *not* just because it's cheap. Remember the old saying, which I just made up, "Two dollars here, two dollars there, soon you're out four dollars." And four dollars times fifty is enough to have your zeppelin polished three times. Now let's charge forward in our quest for poker knowledge.

COURSE LESSON 18

FOURTH STREET
TRIPS

If you started with three-of-a-kind and haven't improved, you'll want to stay in anyhow. (Your only improvement on fourth street would be to four-of-a-kind.) You probably still have the best hand. If you are first to act, bet—the maximum in a spread-limit game. You want to discourage players who have made four-straights or four-flushes from drawing to those hands. They will most likely stay anyway, but make them pay for the draw. Don't give them a free chance to beat you. Free cards are good to get, not good to give.

If someone has bet ahead of you, just call, unless there are two or three players yet to act after you who look like they have made four-straights or four-flushes.

In that case, raise. Try to drive them out and narrow the field. While it's true that you do have a good chance of making a full house and winning a big pot if they also make their hands, it's also true that, with several of them drawing to those hands, you stand a higher chance of being beaten if you don't fill up.

If you are the high board but not showing a face

card with your trips here at fourth street, bet the maximum. You don't want to miss any bets here. You won't be tipping the strength of your hand. If they are small trips and you raised at third street, your opponents (those who think of it at all at these medium and lower limits) will most likely have put you on a big pair at third street and, because they see no improvement here at fourth street, will figure that a big pair is still your maximum holding. Remember, most players are going to call at fourth street unless they have drawn a hopeless card.

If another player (*one* player) now has a pair showing whose rank is higher than your trips, your job is to figure out if he has trips, two pair, or has added a pair to his drawing hand. What action did he take at third street? Did he raise showing a card bigger than your trips? He probably has trips larger than yours. Do you want to chase him? Not me.

Of the three possible outcomes, two will be bad for you. If neither of you improves, he wins. If you both improve to full houses, he wins. If you improve and he doesn't, you win. One out of three outcomes in your favor. Can't pay the rent that way.

If *two or more* players have paired their doorcards, the ranks of which are higher than your trips, you are probably beaten in at least one spot. If a raising war develops, you are probably better off giving up your hand—a tough thing to do, but if you're beat, you're beat. It's a judgment call that you can only learn from studying the game, getting to know your opponents, and gaining experience. Mostly experience—and that's something I can't give you. In my years of playing, I've sometimes had to lay down trips in this situation. Only once did I discover that I had tossed the winning hand. So I am financially way ahead on the play.

In the same scenario as the one above, if your trips are higher than the ranks your opponents are showing, raise—and don't stop raising until the maximum amount of raises has been reached, or until you run out of chips. You have the best hand and the ability to drive out the straight and flush draws. If you win it right here at fourth street, fine. If the other trips stay with you, fine. Either way, you have the best of it.

You should usually play trips aggressively at fourth street unless you find a specific reason not to.

In fixed-limit games at public poker, a player showing a pair at fourth street has the option of making a single fourth-street bet, or of making the double fifth-street bet. For example, in a $5-$10 game, you could bet either $5 or $10 on fourth street with an open pair. Most players will do one or the other, the same way each time. Good players tend toward making the double bet. Don't *you* tend toward anything—think first.

If you pair your doorcard and now have four-of-a-kind, whether you check, bet, or make it the double-bet depends on several factors: the value of your cards (how big they are); how many players you're against; who those players are (good or bad); and, primarily, on what action will look most natural.

If you were the low card on third street showing a three in an unraised pot, and have caught another three here on fourth street, it would look perfectly natural to check. Your opponents probably will assume that you hold only the two threes you are showing which, if that's all you have, you wouldn't bet. Your slow play looks *natural*.

Most players, especially the good ones who know what a long shot four-of-a-kind is, will be much more likely to put you on trips than on quads. If you check into a large field, you'll probably get a bet from someone. Even if you don't, you've given all these nice people a chance to catch up and make something, so that you can make some money.

If you have *raised* at third street with your small trips, or just called a raise, and have now caught another card of your rank here at fourth street, your opponents will most likely put you on two big pair or on small trips. Whether you bet the single or double bet still depends on the factors listed above.

Here's an example from the other end of the scale: Suppose you started with *big* trips, three kings, and have caught the fourth king here at fourth street. Now your board shows a pair of kings. Single bet or double bet?

**In this spot, what looks most
natural can cost you money.**

The most natural looking move would be the

double bet, announcing that you're trying to win it right now. But of course you're not. You want customers. To bet any amount would drive off those customers. But to check would look like you're obviously trying to trap them—which, of course, you are. But that's really your only option. Give them a free card and hope someone catches up enough to give you a play.

Suppose you did start with a pair of threes and now catch a third three at fourth street. Play the same as if you had *started* with trip threes at third street and haven't improved on fourth street. Against a large field, bet or raise the maximum (if you have an option in a spread-limit game) and try to reduce the competition. You want to drive out any opponent who is considering staying with a medium pair. You won't be able to get a large pair out, but get out those you can chase out with aggressive betting. ♠

COURSE LESSON 19

FOURTH STREET
HIGH PAIRS

What's the difference—hidden pair or split pair? Surprise value and amount of return on your money invested with a hidden pair.

To call a raise in either situation will cost you the same amount of money. But when you improve your *hidden* pair to trips, your opponent won't be able to see that, and will continue to play. When you improve the *split* pair by pairing your doorcard, your hand is transparent and your opponent probably will fold. So in the first instance, you figure to make a lot more money than in the second instance, but it costs you the same amount either way. You get a better return on your investment for the same amount of money.

Most players at these limits routinely fold when an opponent pairs his doorcard, fearing trips. That's a good, healthy fear. But don't fold automatically. Whether you play or fold depends on the value of his (possible) trips, and the size and liveliness of your pair.

Let's suppose that you started at third street with a hidden pair of jacks in a raised pot. The raise came from a ten and you're fairly certain, because of the other cards showing on the board and because of your knowledge of your opponent, that he has a pair of tens. Another player calls, showing a four. You know that if he had three fours, he would have raised or reraised at third street. He now catches another four here on fourth street. His most likely hand is two small pair, with his top pair probably being sevens or eights. Your pair is higher than either of his pairs. If your cards are live, including your kickers, call.

But let's say that a jack raised on third street and a queen reraised. *Remember, players at the middle and lower limits almost always have what they are representing,* so if either of them pairs his doorcard here at fourth street, he most likely has trips. Even if you have a pair of aces, you should pass at these limits, *unless* your cards are all live and his are dead. Then consider taking off another card for the small half-bet here on fourth street. But be aware that you are running uphill. Don't get married to your aces.

Generally speaking, you want to avoid chasing any pair that is higher than your pair *unless* you have a couple of overcards to your opponent's pair, and all of your cards are live while his are not, or your pair is hidden.

You'll even want to show respect for your opponent's overcards. If you started with a pair of queens and have gotten no help here on fourth street, and if your opponent's board now shows an ace and a king, even if you think he doesn't have a pair of either of them, you are not in a good place to show a profit if his cards are live. And if one of your queens is gone, which reduces your chances of making trips, you are most likely about to become a contributor.

If you suspect (or know) that your opponent has two pair while you still have only one pair, you can continue to play if your pair is higher than either of his suspected pairs and if all of your cards are live. Otherwise, fold.

If no one has improved and you figure that your high pair is the best hand, bet the maximum. You'd like to win it right here, or set yourself up to take it with a fifth-street bet if you catch a scare card. If your high pair has improved to trips, see Lesson 18, Fourth Street Trips. ♠

COURSE LESSON 20

FOURTH STREET
TWO PAIR

Two pair is probably the most difficult hand to play in all of poker. Appropriately, two pair and trips are where the most money is won and lost. Any fool can toss a garbage hand, or win with a big hand. It's what you do with your middle-value hands that will determine to a large extent your profit or loss picture. After all, most of the hands you play will be middle-value. The garbage hands you toss away and the big hands don't come along that often.

If you make two pair here at fourth street and if no one is showing a pair higher than either of your pairs, bet or raise the maximum. This hand must be protected! You have a good hand with two pair, but your chances of improvement are not good. Cut down the competition and you stand a better chance of winning the pot. If you drive everyone out and win it right here, that's just fine. Smile and take the money, remembering that it's better to win a small pot than to lose a big one.

**If you are playing two pair
on fourth street, you'll
want two essentials:
live cards and overpairs.**

I want my cards to be absolutely live because I'm a long shot to improve even when my cards *are* live—3.5-to-1 here at fourth street. Not too bad. 5-to-1 on fifth street. Getting worse. *10-to-1 at sixth street.* Bummer! It's beginning to look as though I'd rather not reach sixth street with this hand. We'll see.

Overpairs—I need them so that even if I don't improve, I still will have a shot at winning if my opponent also makes two pair.

Raising with two pair on fourth street for protection is a matter of position, exposed cards, whether you raised on third street, how many players have already called, and the ranks of your two pair.

For example, if you just called on third street with a split pair of sevens and a four as a sidecard, you have a seven showing with a four and a seven down. You catch another four, giving you sevens and fours. The high board is to your left and bets. Four players call by the time the action gets to you. Do you raise? Well, "depends." What's your objective? Protection. You probably won't be able to accomplish that objective. With five other players having already put in a bet, you probably won't be able to drop enough of them. Fold.

If the high board is immediately to your *right* and bets, your raise would now have a chance of accomplishing your objective of protecting your hand. Anyone who comes in behind you must call two bets *cold,* instead of just the one bet. But it's either raise or fold—*no call here!* If you are reraised, you'll have to fold. Someone has trips or two big pair. Read the board.

If he checks, do you bet? Not with a *small* two pair. Take a free card or fold.

If you have made two *big* pair—if you started with a split pair of medium value, with a king as your sidecard (no third-street raise), and you catch a king here at fourth street—you'll have an easier time playing your hand. You'll look stronger and you'll *be* stronger. (Keep reading the board.)

If you make two pair, but your opponent pairs his doorcard and bets, you must either fold or raise. Calling would be your worst move. If his exposed pair is higher than either of your two pair, fold. If it isn't, then you have an overpair on him and should raise the maximum. If he reraises, you must give some consideration to his having trips.

If he just calls, you have no further specific information and must play cautiously. This is one of those spots where knowledge of your opponent can be very helpful in determining what his raise or call means. Remember, there is no substitute for knowledge of your opponents. If it appears that you both have two pair, make sure that yours is the higher two pair. And make sure that your cards are live.

To reiterate, two pair is the most difficult hand to play in all of poker. If you are going to play such a hand, you must play it *fast.* Bet or raise the maximum. If you're not willing to play fast, that's okay, but release the hand.

**At medium and lower limits, do not
limp in with two pair on fourth street or
you won't like what usually happens
to you on seventh street.**

So here's another worthwhile repeat: Two pair
must be protected, because, although it is probably
the best hand at the moment, it's not likely to
improve. Play it fast.

Here's a tidbit of information that will be
helpful somewhere down the line, possibly even in
one of the above problems. A player who raises at
fourth street is more likely to have two pair than
three-of-a-kind. Most players with trips just call at
fourth street in an attempt to keep players in.

Let's now suppose that both you and your
opponent have made two pair on fourth street. You
hold jacks and sevens while you strongly suspect
(or know) that your opponent has queens and tens.
How are you going to play this hand? If you're
smart, you won't. Again, of the three things that can
happen, two will be bad for you. If neither of you
improves, you lose. If you both improve, you lose. If
you improve and your opponent doesn't, you win.

How about your two pair against your
opponent's *one* pair, which is higher than either
of your pair? At first glance it looks good. But at
second glance, you don't like it. With three cards to
come, your opponent can pair *any one* of his cards,
or make trips of his pair, and your two pair will go

down the tubes.

You should be getting a clear picture that two small pair is something of a death hand.

Such a hand is so easily outdrawn that it's a long-range money loser. It's death against two higher pair and, as we have seen, it has little life against even *one* higher pair on fourth street. ♠

COURSE LESSON 21

FOURTH STREET
MEDIUM AND SMALL PAIRS

If you started with a medium or small pair and have received no improvement, you must play with caution, if at all. But automatically folding is not correct. You can continue to play, but you'll need other values with your live pair.

If you perceive that your opponent is on a big pair, which would have to be higher than yours, you must have a couple of live overcards to his pair to call a bet.

But if there is a raise from any player, you're done with it. Yes, you see the bigger kids at the higher limits ram and jam with these cards, but if you try it at the lower limits, the only jammin' you'll keep doing is your hand into your pocket to get more money.

If your hand with the live medium pair has three suited cards that are live, be inclined to call for the half-bet here on fourth street.

If your pair has improved to trips or a high two-pair, see the preceding Lessons 18 and 20 in those categories.

Just a reminder: A low two pair must be played with caution, if at all. Fives and threes is just not much of a poker hand, unless you can determine that it is the best at the moment. Then push it as hard as you can. Try to win with it right here, *or give it up if it looks like you can't.* ♠

COURSE LESSON 22

FOURTH STREET
THE DRAWING HANDS

If you started with three to a straight flush and didn't get *any* improvement (to a four-straight, a four-flush, a four-straight-flush, or by pairing a big card), you can consider staying for another round *if* you have an overcard or two in your hand. But if it's going to cost more than one bet, pass, whether you have overcards or not.

If you do catch a fourth card to your straight flush, and if your needed cards are still live, you'll be thinking in terms of going all the way to the end. But again, don't get all bent out of shape about getting a straight flush. Remember, there are only two cards in the whole deck that can make your hand.

If a couple of players have paired their doorcards and the action gets heavy, you'll be tempted to think that you can beat these guys when they make their full houses because you have a straight flush. Not yet, and unlikely. Think instead in terms of how you'll play the hand if it develops into a flush or a straight. Now do you want to go against the possibility of one or two full houses? If you think "yes," we'll try to change your mind when we get to those lessons.

7 CARD STUD

In a multi-way hand (and most hands at these limits are multi-way), if the action is checked to you in late position, put in the maximum bet if you have an option in a spread-limit game. If you win it right here, that's Okay. If you get callers, that's okay too.

In the same position, if there is a bet, just call if there will be a couple of other players in the pot, giving you good pot odds. But if it's going to be just you against what looks like a big pair, raise the maximum. You'd like to win it right here and not have to play a drawing hand heads up.

If it's bet and raised to you, think in terms of what you perceive you'll have to beat and whether you can beat it with your second-best outcome (which is your most likely outcome).

If you are in early position in a multi-way hand, go ahead and bet. You're hoping for callers, but if you get a raise, be guided again by what you think you'll have to beat, and whether you believe you can beat the raiser with your second-best outcome.

If you are heads up against a player who has a big pair, you are a bit of a dog. You must improve to win. If you think that a bet or raise will win the pot right now, go for it. If you are heads up against a player who is also on a drawing hand, play selectively aggressive (*see Lesson 30*).

If you pair a high card, begin thinking of that as your primary hand, especially if some of your needed suit have also appeared around the board. If you pair a low card, think seriously about folding, unless your sidecards are overcards, and all of your cards are live. If you improve to a four-flush or four-straight, see the following lessons.

A mistake many otherwise good players make is automatically folding when they start with a three-flush and don't catch another suited card to make a four-flush on fourth street.

Flush Draws. There are other reasons to continue with the hand. If you now have a pair, especially a high pair that figures to be the biggest pair; if your needed cards (pair cards and suit cards) are still live; and if you now also have a three-straight combined with your three-flush (also live... always live. I'll say it again, seven-card stud is a game of *live* cards).

But if you haven't added *any* values to your hand, and if you still hold only a three-flush, give it up. The odds against catching the flush are 8.5-to-1. And if you don't make the four-flush at fifth street, the odds will go to 23-to-1.

When you do make a four-flush at fourth street, the chances of making the flush are excellent: only 1.25-to-1 against. You will most likely be staying to the end, unless one of your opponents is showing something such as two pair or trips, in which case you are in danger of making the flush and having it beaten.

7 CARD STUD

A couple more reasons to decline further participation are if an opponent pairs his doorcard and appears to have made trips, or if you see too many of your needed suit cards on the board. It's still a maximum of three for a quality flush draw, and two for a non-quality flush draw.

But if all factors are favorable and you do continue, do your checking, betting, and raising in such a way that you don't establish a pattern which can be read by your more astute opponents. Most players fall into one of two categories when it comes to betting or raising with four-flushes. Either they never bet or raise a four-flush, or they always do. Either way, they soon become easy to read. So if I know that you bet your flush only after you've made it, why should I ever call you in that instance—unless I can beat you? Mix up your play with a tendency towards aggressiveness. Keep your opponents off-balance.

Straight Draws. If you started with a 9-10-J or 10-J-Q, and didn't get any improvement to a four-straight or by pairing a high card, you're finished with it unless you can play for free.

If you catch a card that now gives you an inside straight draw, exercise your discipline. What often happens to players with this kind of very marginal improvement is that the little voice of the repressed gambler that lives in their mind whispers, "We've improved. Let's keep playing." Ignore that voice. That draw is a long-range loser. An exception would be if you now also have three-to-a-flush and an overcard to the board. You can call if someone bets, but you can't call a bet and a raise.

Much of what you have learned about staying with busted straight-flush draws or with busted flush draws, you can also apply to busted straight draws. When the drawing hand you are on goes bust, consider what other values you have with which to continue play; for example, pairing a high card. But don't just be looking for excuses to continue play.

Hold your discipline. Play when you have a positive expectation. Run when you don't.

Now, let's move on to the happier prospect of making a four-straight here on fourth street. Your first thought should be, "Are my cards still live?" The "rule of two points" is still to be considered.

Your next concern should be whether your opponents have caught something dangerous-looking such as a big open pair which could be trips or two big pair. You don't want to make your straight and then run into a full house. It's a real bear to work your way through a maze of strategy, remembering a board full of your opponents' exposed and turned-over cards, only to have your stack of chips look like it got stomped by an elephant after the showdown. And you can be sure that does happen.

Pay attention, or you'll be paying off your opponents.

If those dangers are not present, you will probably keep playing to the river, or until something dangerous does show up. Mostly, tend to just call with your four-straight unless you are in late position with some power cards showing.

If you think you can either steal the pot now, or set up a steal on the next card, put in a raise. That would be a semi-bluff, which is betting or raising with what you figure is not the best hand, but there are more cards coming that can make your hand. A total bluff is when there are no more cards coming and you can only win if you bet and your opponents fold.

It is very helpful to know who you can steal from—and who you can't.

Here is another instance where knowledge of your opponents is important—remember, there is no substitute for it.

The purpose of your tendency to just call when your only value is a drawing hand is to keep players in so that you will be getting the proper pot odds to draw to the hand.

If you started on third street with overcards only, you will want to have paired one of them before calling any fourth-street bets. If you do pair, see Lesson 19.

One of my boyhood idols was a college basketball player named Ed McCauley. They called him "Easy Ed." He was an All-American center at the University of St. Louis, and later became a star in the NBA.

ROY WEST · CARDOZA PUBLISHING

One of my favorite quotations is from Easy Ed:

**"When you are not practicing,
someone, somewhere, is practicing.
And when you meet, he will beat you."**

The application to poker is obvious. Get busy. ♠

Fifth Street Strategy

Introduction

Whether to get involved in the pot on third street is your most important decision at seven-card stud. Of close second importance is whether you continue to play at fifth street. It is here that the betting will tend to become heavier in a spread-limit game, and the limits will double in a fixed-limit game. And on fifth street, players either have made their hands or now have a holding to which they can draw to make a completed hand. Possibilities abound. With this in mind, keep in mind the following "rule of play":

7 CARD STUD

Don't stay past fifth street unless you are planning to stay to the end.

Now let's talk about what to stay with.

COURSE LESSON 23

FIFTH STREET
TRIPS

If you started with three-of-a-kind and have now made a full house or, wonder of wonders, four-of-a-kind, you can afford to lay back a bit—slow play. You are an almost certain winner and don't want to run off your customers. Just call any bets in front of you, of if you are first to act, go ahead and bet. It would be a mistake to go for a check-raise here, but many players do just that. You will have tipped the strength of your hand too early, and will have given your opponents an opportunity to fold without contributing heavily to your bankroll.

If the game allows for an option as to how much you can bet (a spread-limit game), I recommend three-quarters of the allowable maximum bet. Don't get cute and bet the minimum. Your board will be showing at least one pair, and all but the least sophisticated of players will see through your little trap.

Just call any raises, but don't reraise—not yet. Wait for sixth street to set the hook. At fifth street, it's too easy for your opponents to let go of their hands, even drawing hands. They haven't invested much yet and don't feel compelled to "protect" their money. Of course, *you* should never feel that you must protect the money you have put in. Once it's in the pot, it's no longer yours. It belongs to the pot and requires no protection. Your only reason for continuing to play a hand is if it has a good chance to win: You have either the best hand or the best draw.

If you haven't improved your trips, you still have a strong hand. But you must be aware of players who have now paired with cards that rank higher than your trips, especially if they have paired their doorcards. It is now possible that they have trips which are higher than yours. But if both their third-street and fourth-street upcards are suited, it is quite possible that they have been drawing to a four-flush and have now added a pair. This gives them a powerful draw. You must bet or raise as much as you can in an effort to drive them out, or to make them pay the maximum to try to beat your holding. You are still a favorite, but if you could win it right here, a sigh of relief would be in order.

Here's a piece of information you may find interesting and useful:

An opponent who pairs his fourth-street card is more likely to have two pair than three-of-a-kind.

But if the rank of his exposed pair is higher than your trips, you'd rather have him out. If his hand is two-pair, you have him beaten. But if you both make full houses, his will be higher than yours (if he fills it with his higher pair rather than his other pair), and you'll lose a lot of chips learning that.

With two cards yet to come, your odds are good for making a full house (2.5-to-1), so you'll be staying to the end. But continue to watch the board for the cards you need, and for the cards that you figure your opponents need. If your needed cards are gone, and if you're getting a lot of action from players showing three-to-a-flush while their cards are still live, you could be drawing dead. It's very tough to throw away three-of-a-kind; use your best judgment here.

What I'm giving you with this Course is about ninety percent of what Las Vegas professionals use at these medium and lower limits. The rest is experience and judgment. That I can't give you.

If you perceive no threatening competition, play your trips as aggressively as you can, especially against several players. Someone is drawing to something. You'd rather deny them that opportunity. Against one player who probably is still in with just a pair, you can lay back a bit. ♠

COURSE LESSON 24

FIFTH STREET
PAIRS

If you have reached fifth street with no improvement of your one big pair, whether you continue playing is determined mostly by the same factors you had to consider on fourth street: overcards and live cards. Don't automatically fold, as many players do in this spot. Think first. You can carefully consider staying if there are no more than two players remaining in contention for the pot. But with three or more active players, the chances of your big pair holding up diminish.

If it appears that your opponent has made two pair while you still have only one big pair, you can keep playing if your pair is higher than his biggest pair and your cards are live.

Let's say that you started with a pair of kings and your third-street raise was called by an obvious pair of queens. Neither of you improved at fourth street. Now on fifth street, the queens have added a pair of nines. Since your kings are higher than either of his two-pair, play on if your cards are live. But if the queens now have a pair of aces to go with them, you are done, live cards or not, because one of his pairs is bigger than your pair.

There are times to chase and there are times to run. The primary determining factors are overpairs, overcards, and live cards. ♠

COURSE LESSON 25

FIFTH STREET
TWO PAIR

If you have two pair here at fifth street, it is important to maintain your requirements for overpairs and live cards. Many players will continue with two smaller pair against their opponent's one bigger pair (which we saw at fourth street is not such a good idea) if they now have added a live overcard to their hands. To me, that's a stretch. I haven't added that much strength to a hand that I have to play fast, betting and raising as much as I can to try to eliminate opponents.

The positive factor is that this is the place, here at fifth street where the bets double in a structured game, where you have your best chance of running off that player who holds one higher pair.

Here's where knowledge of your opponents pays off once again. Will he run, or will he stay if you push hard? I'd make my decision to play aggressively, or fold, on that basis.

You want to be either the bettor or the raiser, not a caller, with your two pair on fifth street—just as on fourth street. ♠

COURSE LESSON 26

FIFTH STREET
THE DRAWING HANDS

If you haven't completed your straight-flush here at fifth street, the information from the fourth street lesson still applies: Three hands are still possible—the straight flush, a flush, or a straight. Just *how* possible depends on how many of your needed cards you've seen around the board. You have been carefully watching the board, right? Of course!

If your *four-straight* or *four-flush* is still a four-straight or four-flush, you can continue play *if* your needed cards are still live. But if you have four spades and you've seen five other spades on the board, the odds are long. Give it up. If you've seen a maximum of three other spades while drawing to a quality flush, or two others if you are drawing to a non-quality flush, play on.

If you're drawing to an open-end straight, you still should take into consideration "the rule of two points."

But there's more to consider than just how many of your cards are still live and available. After you've satisfied that requirement, you'll want to determine whether your straight or flush will win if you make it.

7 CARD STUD

Stay out of the trap of drawing to the second-best (or even third-best) drawing hand. That's a big money loser for a lot of players.

For example, if your four-flush is jack-high and other players are drawing to (or have made) queen or king-high flushes here at fifth street, you should give up your flush draw—but most players don't. They continue blindly, not even realizing they are in danger of making the hand and *then losing*. Or if they realize that their flush draw is smaller, they are hoping to catch bigger and win. That's a lot of hoping—and gambling. Save your money for a potentially more profitable spot.

The same goes for your straight draws. If you determine that others are drawing to flushes, or even bigger straights, you should withdraw and wait for an easier battle.

Remember, we talked earlier about playing with the best hand or with the best draw. In the situations above, you have neither. What you have is the danger of making your hand and losing. Get it clear in your mind that it's never a good idea to be trying for the second-best drawing hand—and be alert enough to realize when you are doing it. And stop. In order for you to win, you must make your hand while your opponent misses his. Your only other win is if you both miss, but you have the highest cards, or if you stumble into a pair on the end.

Often times, instead of filling your flush at fifth street, you will pair a big card and have an overpair such as kings.

You might now have the best hand and the best draw. You can play this hand aggressively.

If it's checked to you, bet. If it's already bet, raise. If you narrow the field to one opponent, that's okay. Your most likely winning hand is the pair of kings. It's also okay if you have two or three callers to give you good pot odds for your flush draw.

This fifth street raise often will allow you to get through seventh street at no additional cost. Usually, you will be checked to on sixth street. If you improve to two pair, trips, or make your drawing hand there, bet. If not, you can try for the semi-bluff bet and hope to win right there, or you can check along and take a free seventh street card.

Also, that fifth-street raise will usually assure you of having only one opponent at sixth street, making for a greater likelihood of your pair standing up.

If you don't have that big pair to go with your flush draw on fifth street, you won't want to be quite as aggressive with the hand, unless you are fairly certain that a semi-bluff bet will win for you right here. Otherwise, call any bets that are made, or check along and take the free card.

If you have made a straight or flush on fifth street, I suggest pushing the hand hard at these limits.

Bet or raise as much as you can to protect the hand. This is your hand to the end. It can become a little higher straight or flush, but that's it. A player with two small pair can make a full house in the next two cards. A player with just one pair can trip up, or make two pair at sixth street, and then fill up on seventh street. Discourage them from trying. Make it as expensive as you can for them to draw to those hands.

Keep in mind that after receiving the fifth card, the betting will tend to become heavier in spread-limit games, or will double in fixed-limit games. It is at this point that players have either made their hands or have a holding to which they can draw and make a completed hand.

Given this information, you would do well to keep this "rule of play" in mind: Don't stay past fifth street unless you are planning to stay to the end. Your hand should be strong enough here that folding on sixth street becomes a rarity. ♠

Sixth Street Strategy

Introduction

When you (and your opponents) have paid for a sixth card, you have generally committed yourself to the end. Therefore, you should have either a good hand already made, or a draw to a good hand.

You can now become more aggressive with a completed hand. Your opponents have more of a commitment to the pot, and will probably be going all the way.

Now let's look at three types of sixth-street hands: super-powerful, weak, and middle-good.

7 CARD STUD

Super-Powerful Hands. If you have a super-powerful hand (such as a straight flush, four-of-a-kind, or a big full house), and you are first to act, try to determine from your opponents' upcards and from your knowledge of your opponents, whether checking or betting will make you the most money. Many players always check in this spot; others always bet. Don't do anything automatically. Bet if you have only one opponent and you think he will call. But if you believe that your bet will cause him to fold, check. You don't want to lose your only customer. Give him a chance to catch up.

Give more consideration to checking if you have several opponents, especially if you believe that another early-position player will do the betting if you check. If the player to your left bets and several players call before the action gets back to you, you can now put in a raise. Your opponents have further committed themselves to the pot, and have made it that much more difficult to get away from their hands, whether they are still drawing or already have made a hand. The advantage to a check-raise here on sixth street is that there is one more card to come and your opponents are still hoping to make their hands. You have a good chance of getting a call from a four-flush on sixth street, but (obviously) you have no chance of getting a call from that hand on seventh street if he doesn't complete it.

If everyone checks along, you have missed a bet, yes, but if no one can bet here at sixth street, they probably don't have enough to call with either. You've given them a chance to make something at seventh street, and give you a play so that you can win a few more bets.

Weak Hands. If you hold a weak hand—you have not improved your starting hand (except for trips or the highest pair)—you should be gone, unless you have been able to play this far for free. If your opponents, with slightly stronger hands, have been giving you free cards, they have been making mistakes. If you have been giving free cards with the best hand because it wasn't a strong hand, *you* have been making the mistakes. With the best hand, get your chips into the pot. Do not give free cards.

Middle-Good Hands. If you have a middle-good hand, such as a flush, a straight, trips, or two big pair, evaluate your opponents' hands. If you think that your hand is the best, push it hard. If you have a good hand that you suspect might not be the best hand, and you are reluctant to throw it away, try to reach the showdown as cheaply as possible.

A raising war between two other opponents who are each showing pairs could very well mean that at least one of them has a full house. You might have to toss your middle-good hand. Use your best judgment—gather information to make a decision. And remember to take knowledge of your opponents into account.

If you have four-to-a-flush or four-to-a-straight with live cards, you'll want to play to the end, unless it is obvious that you'll be beaten even if you do make the hand. A player showing four-to-a-flush here at sixth street with higher cards than yours either has you beaten already, or has a draw to a hand that will beat you if he makes it. Have you been watching the board so that you *know* how many of his cards, and how many of your cards, are still available?

The farther along you progress with a hand, the more important a study of the board becomes. You should know which cards have shown and which have been turned over.

The only three ways to acquire this skill are: Practice, practice, practice! The very best time to practice is when you are not involved in a hand. Instead of watching whatever sporting event is on TV or checking out your keno ticket, stay into the game. When it's obvious from your first three cards at third street that you are not going to play the hand, start putting intense concentration into remembering the exposed cards as your opponents fold them. This process will soon become automatic. (There's more on remembering cards in Lesson 3.) And remain alert: You cannot remember a card you have not seen.

A two-pair hand is unlikely to improve on the seventh card, yet it has a fair chance to win an average pot, but not usually a big pot, at these limits. A big pot got big because big hands have been competing for it. A raise probably will no longer protect your hand at this point. Strong betting action from an opponent showing a pair higher than either of your pairs makes even a call a doubtful proposition.

If you have been playing all along with one pair, two pair, or trips against one opponent who has just been calling—and now he gets a third suited card here at sixth street and either bets or raises—look to see if his doorcard is the same suit as the one he has just caught. If so, he probably has made a flush. A player who makes a flush usually makes it in the suit of his doorcard. If he hasn't made a flush, he probably has made two pair or trips and is trying to win the pot right now. Call if you have a good *live* draw to a hand that will beat him. Raise if you figure that you have the best hand.

> **If you find yourself throwing away a lot of hands on sixth street, you are doing something wrong at both fifth and sixth streets.**

You aren't really strong enough to stay at fifth street, but you are probably telling yourself, "I'll see just one more card, and if I don't make this hand, I'll fold." But then if you don't make it at sixth street, it's easy to tell yourself the same thing again, because there is only one more card to come—so you might as well see it, too ("I've come this far. Might as well go all the way"). Then you will usually find yourself paying off a better hand at seventh street.

It should be a rare occurrence for you to throw away a hand on sixth street. The pot will most likely be offering good enough odds for you to play, even if you are a slight dog. An exception would be if you are now beaten strongly in sight, or if your needed cards are now showing all over the board. For example, you have a straight or a flush, or a draw to one of those hands, but two players, each showing pairs, have started a raising war. The probability is high that one of them has a full house. Or suppose you have two pair but an opponent has now made open trips, especially if they are higher than both of your pairs. If you don't make a full house at seventh street, you lose. And if you both make full houses, his will be higher than yours.

Your sixth-street hand is more than likely going to be your seventh-street hand, too. So play it that way, unless it's a monster and you're trying to keep your customers in the hand to the end. ♠

Seventh Street Strategy

Introduction

It is on seventh street that your close attention to the details of the game all through the hand will pay off. By being able to recall the cards that have been folded, you have valuable information about the possibilities of your opponents' hand—and you have an advantage over the guesser. Remember, make decisions based on information you have gathered all during the play of the hand. If you are guessing, you are gambling. Take the gamble out of your game.

On seventh street, you probably won't get any more information about your opponents' hands because the last card is dealt face down. So when the final card is dealt, you should be looking at your opponents rather than at the cards being dealt, like most other players will be doing. Don't even look at your own last card until you have watched your opponents look at theirs. Your card isn't going anywhere. It'll still be there when you're ready to look.

This is an excellent spot to pick up a tell from an opponent who has been drawing to a flush or a straight.

Many times, after a player has missed his hand, he will allow a *slight* look of disgust to *briefly* cross his face; his shoulders might sag *a bit*; or he may become visibly disinterested in the hand. He might even share his misfortune with the friendly player next to him, in which case he did not make the hand. If you had made such a hand, would you show it to anyone? Certainly not. You'd be concerned that he would show a tell to give it away. However, if his wife walks up to the game at that point and he shows *her* his hand, he has made it. "See, honey, what a terrific player I am!"

If he looks for only a very short time, folds his cards together and glances at his chips, he has made the hand and is ready to call any bets.

If he looks at his hole cards and then at his upcards, and then at his hole cards, and again at his upcards, like many recreational players do, he is most likely trying to figure out if he made a straight.

It doesn't take that much looking, even for a novice, to see if he made a flush or a full house. If you are watching the seventh card you are being dealt, you'll miss all of this.

After all the cards have been dealt and four or more players are still active in the hand, you can figure it will take, *on average,* three eights or better to win at these limits. With three or fewer players staying to the end, two big pair will win more often than they will lose.

Keep in mind that a big pot got big here because of big hands competing for it. And the bigger the pot, the bigger the hand you usually need to win it.

**Straightforward play is usually
your best course of action
on seventh street at these limits.**

Check-raising is seldom a paying proposition. Most of your opponents are not sophisticated enough even to be trapped. Your "moves" will be wasted. Forget the tricky stuff. That's not what gets the money at these limits. Solid, mistake-free play sends you to the cashier on your way home, instead of directly out the door.

If you think you have the best hand and are first to act, go ahead and bet. Many players will *call* with a hand they would not *bet,* because they are suspicious of a bluff and believe it is a mark of dishonor to be bluffed out. Bet your strong hands, trips or better, and try to reach an inexpensive showdown with your medium or weak hands. But keep in mind that if you perceive that yours is the best hand, whatever its strength, bet it. Remember: You don't always need a *big* hand, just the *best* hand.

If you find yourself in the position of having to make your best guess as to whether yours is the best hand, it usually is better to call for one last bet with your average-to-good hand, rather than trying to outguess yourself. The pot will most likely be offering you good enough odds that you need to be right only one-out-of-five times to make this a profitable play. This is a defensive call that should be made when you have genuine doubt about having the best hand, but there is still a good possibility that you do.

As an example, suppose you are against one player whom you have figured to be on a flush draw. You have three sevens. At sixth street, he was showing four spades as his board. You've seen only two other spades. You watch as he looks at his last card, but you don't get a tell. You are high and check. He bets, representing the flush. Rather than trying to guess, and wonder, and figure out if he has made it, just call. It's only one more bet. If he has made it, you pay him off. If he hasn't, you win a nice pot.

Keep in mind that this is a defensive call that should be made when you have genuine doubt, but still have a possibility, about having the best hand.

An added bonus is that your call will keep players from bluffing at you, especially if you have a conservative image. But do use your best judgment. Be careful that you don't allow yourself to become a calling station.

Many players, even smart players, fold too often in such situations. The pot is usually large enough at seventh street, even heads up, that it isn't worth your energy to try to guess whether to call or fold. If you figure that you only *might* have the best hand, call. This assumes that there is not the threat of a raise from a third player in the pot. Even if your call is a mistake, it can cost you only one more bet. *Not* making this call when you should will cost you a whole pot.

What about bluffing? My advice at these limits is simple and specific—don't. It is generally a losing play. If the pot is big, you aren't going to bluff everyone out of it for one more bet. And if it's a small pot, why are you bluffing at it?

Conventional poker wisdom says that you must advertise by doing some bluffing early in order to get paid off on your big hands later. This assumes that you are going to *have* big hands later. You might not. But here's my basic reasoning:

I make a distinction between bluffing in a home game and bluffing at public poker. What's the difference? Simple...

If you have been playing every Friday night with the same bunch of people for several years, you *must* do some bluffing. Otherwise, even the slowest of them will eventually figure out that you don't bluff, and they will tend not to call your seventh street bets unless they hold big hands which can beat you.

In public poker, at these medium and lower limits, bluffing isn't necessary. In fact, it is quite difficult to establish a reputation as a bluffer. That's because you aren't playing against the same players at every session. To become known as a bluffer, logically enough, you have to attempt, and get caught at, *several* unsuccessful bluffs. That costs money. But before you can really set up your image as a bluffer, two opponents leave for dinner, a third goes broke, and a fourth runs off to catch a plane. Their places are taken by players who have not seen you bluff, so you have to start the process all over. Very expensive advertising.

Another problem with bluffing these people is that they tend to do a lot of calling on seventh street, even if you raise or check-raise.

At these limits, the majority of the time, you must show down the best hand to win, because most hands do go to a showdown.

On the other side of the coin, there is a poker adage which states, "Give the bluffers a chance to bluff." That means that if you are heads-up against a known bluffer while you are holding a strong, hidden hand, and if you suspect that the bluffer has a weak hand that he won't call with, don't bet. Check, and give him the opportunity to bluff. If he does, you profit at least one bet by calling; and maybe (but doubtful) two by raising—but only if he suspects that your raise is a bluff. Only a bluffer would suspect this because of his own propensity to bluff. ♠

Roy's Rule #1

Introduction

No Course on winning poker created by me would be complete without a penetrating look at "Roy's Rule #1."

Those of you who have been reading my work over the years know about this important concept and can skip on. For you who are experiencing my teaching for the first time, draw close and listen up.

COURSE LESSON 27

Roy's Rule #1

There are many "Roy's Rules," but only one has a number. Roy's Rule #1 states: *"Play Happy Or Don't Play."*

Ignoring this Rule could be hazardous to your bankroll and, more importantly, to your peace of mind.

Some readers will merely scan the pages of this Course, looking for specific tips and information on how to best play the game of seven-card stud. Anything else is of little interest to them. If you are one of these readers, reconsider. Be interested. Keep reading. This is quite probably the most important playing advice outside of strategy that I can give you. It is more of the "stuff" of winning poker. I believe it has universal application.

Roy's Rule # 1, "Play Happy Or Don't Play," is truly my number one consideration when playing poker.

You've seen players getting angry—cursing, throwing cards. Obviously, they are in no condition to play. But they remain in the game while their proficiency deteriorates. They think they're playing as well as ever. They aren't.

There are several terms for this condition: "going on tilt," "getting your nose open," and "steaming." It most often happens when a player is losing. When it happens to you, you should leave the game. You should, but you probably won't.

Play happy or don't play. That doesn't mean you have to be joking and laughing and slapping people on the back. But you should be able to approach the game with a pleasant attitude. If you're unhappy about your situation, why do you stay in it? To get the money? Fat chance!

When you're playing unhappy, you aren't playing your best game, especially if you're unhappy because you are losing. You start reaching—playing lesser hands—or chasing, most often against a player who has given you a beat. You're going to show *him* a thing or two about poker. More likely, unless you get very lucky, he's going to show *you* another winning hand and take even *more* of your money.

Remember, he's not angry. He's probably quite happy with his wins and is playing his usual steady game. You're the one who is chasing with inferior hands against his normal starting values. And while *his* head is on straight and he's playing his best strategy, your mind is too busy being angry to play as well as you know how. You're not alert. You miss things you should see.

You don't have to be in a towering rage for emotions to affect your play. Just being grumpy will do.

Sitting silently while your guts are churning, waiting for your chance at revenge, will bring you to the same place.

Forget being angry at the dealer. Your anger is an attempt to make him feel guilty. He won't. He has dealt 100 times as many hands as you've ever played, and each hand had at least one loser. He knows he's not responsible for the cards you get (or how you play them). In that respect, he could just as well be a robot sitting there distributing cards.

Forget revenge. The other players didn't do anything to you. They just played the cards they got, the best way they knew how, trying to win the money—*the same as you were doing!*

How do you forget the anger, forget the revenge? Release them. And how do you do that? By realizing that your anger, *and its effects,* are in the only location they can be—within your own mind, and nowhere else. *Nowhere* else.

And the only person they are affecting is *you.*

You have a misconception that someone did something to you, unjustly. They didn't. They were just leading their own lives. By correcting this misconception, you release the anger. No attack, no anger. No anger, you have peace of mind. With a peaceful mind, you play better. When you play better, you win more. ♠

"Play Happy Or Don't Play"

More of Roy's Rules for Winning Poker

COURSE LESSON 28

MENTAL PREPARATION

My thinking is that if I don't have time to prepare mentally, I don't have time to play.

Preparation is first; all else follows.

So what do you do, as a poker player, in preparation for playing? Of course you've acquired all the skill and knowledge of the game you can muster. But what about your preparation before each individual session? If you're like most poker players, you walk into the cardroom, put your bottom on a chair, and start drawing cards *without* any mental preparation.

An athlete will do a series of physical warm-up exercises before working out or going into a competition. And more and more athletes are also doing *mental* preparation. Should you, with your money on the table, do any less?

Mental preparation. I refer to that period of time immediately prior to playing. You can study, read all the books, take all the lessons. But if you sit down in a game without being mentally ready, you're giving up an edge to someone who *is* ready.

This isn't to say that you can't be a winner without doing your pregame mental footwork. Obviously, that is just not so. But I am convinced that mental preparation of some kind would greatly benefit most players.

There probably are as many ways of preparing to play as there are players who prepare. Let's look at a bunch.

I know several players who will read a chapter from a poker book or one of my instructional columns published over the years. This gets the mind attuned to poker. While they're driving to the cardroom, they will think about various poker plays, to keep the mind on poker. When they arrive at the game, they are mentally ready.

Another player puts on his stereo headphones and listens to soft, non-melodic music while talking to himself about what a solid, skillful player he is. A woman I know cranks up her stereo and gives the speakers a workout with stirring march music, while giving herself a loud pep talk just prior to leaving for the cardroom. She continues the pep talk during the drive in. It's something to see when you stop next to her at a red light. But this doesn't bother her. She's preparing to win. And she does win.

Another fellow I know stands in front of a mirror and stares himself directly in the eyes while saying over and over, "I am a winner. I am a winner." When he gets to the point of firmly believing it, he heads for the game. He's hard to beat.

I'm not saying that any of this is a substitute for skill, knowledge, and strategy—but it can be a valuable addition for those who choose to use it.

A friend who is a born-again Christian prays for 5-to-10 minutes before playing—not for a winning session, but to play his best, and to serenely accept whatever the outcome may be.

Some players use hypnosis, having a professional hypnotist give them posthypnotic suggestions about their poker playing.

A world-class poker pro told me that he makes it an absolute rule to "sit down feeling good, and mentally ready, or I don't sit down." He meditates before each session he plays.

Here I quote Bobby Knight, head basketball coach at Indiana, after hearing a comment that his teams have the will to win. Knight said, "No, no. We don't have the will to win. We have the will to *prepare* to win." And that includes mental preparation.

I believe that, for most players, if you are not prepared mentally, you are not prepared.

If you are playing just to be playing—because you have nothing better to do, or because there's nothing on TV—I would be willing to place a small wager that you are not a consistent winner. I would suggest using some of your time getting into a winning frame of mind.

I realize that time is an important consideration for most people. It certainly is for me. But I've come to the strong realization that...

**If I don't have time to prepare mentally,
I don't have time to play.
Preparation is first. All else follows.**

Playing time for many people is immediately after work. Whatever your circumstances, I urge you to take at least ten minutes to be alone. Spend these minutes quietly, relaxed, with your eyes closed. Think about your game. Then free your mind of all thoughts. It will be a good break for you, and will go a long way towards a proper mind set.

When I lived in California, my home was in Westlake Village. I played every day in the nearest legal cardroom of my choice, fifty-five miles away. Several times I drove the fifty-five miles only to find that I just didn't feel like playing poker. I wasn't really up for it. So I'd go to the beach, or drive back home.

That's 110 miles round trip without drawing a card. But I knew that was better than pushing myself to play just because I was there. I could, and would, be there again tomorrow. And the game would be waiting for me.

Keep in mind that the game will be there tomorrow and the next day and next week. The game will wait. You can wait. If you can't wait, then it might be a good idea to examine your motives for playing.

I thought of framing the following "rules" in positive terms, but decided that they play stronger as *don'ts*:

- Don't play if our mind is foggy from lack of sleep, or booze, or drugs, legal or illegal.

- Don't play if you are emotionally upset. Resolve your emotional issues and then come to the poker table.

- Don't play if there is something else you'd rather be, or should be, doing. Go and do what must be done. Then play.

- Don't play if you're not feeling physically fit. A cold or a headache will throw you off your game more than you might realize.

- And don't play if you feel pessimistic about the outcome. You'll probably be proven right.

So our rallying cry at this point is: "If we don't have time to prepare mentally, we don't have time to play." ♠

COURSE LESSON 29

THE "SECRETS" OF WINNING POKER

I don't think there are any secrets to winning poker anymore. There were a lot of them several years ago, but now, with everyone and your brother writing articles, columns and books, the "secrets" have all been rather well-exposed. But I'll have a shot at a few secrets of my own as we continue through this Course with the "stuff" of winning poker.

The first is *discipline*, not for any reason other than *it's the most important*. Most players don't believe that. Good! Those are more players for you to beat.

The beginning and end of consistent, winning poker is discipline.

If *you* don't believe that, good. Come play in my game.

Several years ago I was approached in one of our local card emporiums by a young fellow who wanted to know the secret of winning poker. I looked him in the eye and said, "Discipline." He just looked back at me and said, "Well, okay, if you don't want to tell me," and walked away.

Discipline is one of the most important aspects of consistent winning poker. It doesn't matter how good you *can* play; what matters is how good you *do* play.

And it is discipline that will determine how good you do play. Discipline is what makes everything else work.

I know some very knowledgeable poker players who are always borrowing money. They are constantly broke. It's because they don't have the discipline to make their knowledge work for them.

I'll define discipline for our purposes in this Course as "doing what you know should be done— or not doing what you know should not be done." It's the second part that gets most poker players into trouble.

Discipline will decide how well you play—or how badly you play. If you are a solid, skillful player, but today you give up your discipline and play like a sucker, then today you *are* a sucker.

I'll say it again—It doesn't matter how good you *can play;* what matters is how *good you do play.*

It isn't enough to know what to do while playing poker. What's important is doing it!

If you're losing money in a bad game—a game populated with tight, tough, solid players, a game where you stand little chance of recouping your losses—you must have the discipline to quit that game a loser. If you've stuck any appreciable amount of money in *any* kind of game, and you pick up a mediocre hand that you wouldn't play if you were ahead or even, your better judgment will tell you not to play that hand. If you are exercising self-discipline, you won't play it.

Quite often, good players become bad players because they lose their discipline. The best player at the table one day might become the worst player the next day, or the next hour. A player might take a few losses and his discipline disappears. He gets his nose open and starts steamin'. He begins playing long shots, trying to get even. He's lost.

A lot of money has been blown off by good players giving up their discipline.

When you see it happening, you have an opportunity to add to your bankroll. When you see it happening to *you*, save your bankroll. Leave. Rapidly! Get it back and come on back.

It is almost impossible to win consistently without discipline. It is of the utmost importance at any level of play.

Being flat broke is no fun. And the way a poker player gets there most often is by giving up his discipline.

When you're doing something that's wrong, even though you know it's wrong, you've lost your discipline. Usually you tell yourself that you'll do it this time, but next time you'll be good—then you'll play solidly again. You've given up your discipline. It can happen in a hundred different ways—and they'll all cost you money.

Now here's the good news. The more you exercise your discipline, the easier it becomes to exercise it the next time. Discipline does strengthen as you practice it. So the first time you consciously maintain your discipline, it strengthens it for the second time, which strengthens it for the third time—and it builds. The more you maintain your discipline, the stronger it becomes.

If you think about discipline *before* entering the game, it becomes easier to exercise *during* the game. If you lose your stack enough times, your desire to exercise your discipline will increase—and your conscious desire is a major factor. But why wait to go broke? Start now. Yes, now.

You are most likely to give up your discipline when you're upset.

If you maintain your discipline now, it will grow and make it easier for the next time you are tempted to abandon it. And the next. And the next. Practicing discipline makes it stronger.

This all ties in with Roy's Rule #1: "Play Happy Or Don't Play" because your discipline goes when you're upset. So get away from the table. Get back your composure. It will then be easier to get control of your discipline.

You don't have to become completely disciplined right off the bat. Easy does it. Practice it for an hour at a time at first. Determine that you're going to play with absolute discipline (perfect poker) for one hour. Repeat that exercise, lengthening the time span at each attempt. Soon your self-control (discipline) will be automatic. At those times when you do lose it, you will be able to instantly recognize what has happened and take steps to bring it back.

You might be the most knowledgeable poker player north of the Hoover Dam—but if you don't put that knowledge to work at the table, it is of no value. Many players study the game, but when they get to the table, they make the same mistakes over and over. They don't play as well as they could. They don't play up to their potential

It takes only one or two mistakes to book a losing session.

Most players are looking for reasons to play, to get into a hand. Don't *you* be looking for reasons to play. Look for reasons to *not* play. Example: I have a starting hand of a split pair of sixes with a nine kicker, and there are big cards on the board behind me. Or maybe my kicker is bigger, but one of my sixes is out. To make it worse, I'm in early position. I don't mind playing a split pair of sixes in late position with little chance of a raise behind me. But with such a hand I'm looking for reasons to *not* play.

Let me remind you of an old saying I just made up: "Gamble comes along with every hand—value doesn't come along that often."

The quality that makes the biggest difference between a winner and a loser at the game of poker is discipline. To win the most money, you must discipline yourself to throw away the majority of third-street hands dealt to you. Remove from your mind the idea that the big wins go to the players who have created the most brilliant strategies. The consistent winners are those who play solid poker with the fewest mistakes. They are the skillful players who have, in addition to their skill, developed their discipline. Therein lies one of the major "secrets" to winning poker.

The application of all other facets of poker will require discipline. Without discipline you might as well not take the time and effort to develop your game. Application requires—*demands*—discipline. ♠

COURSE LESSON 30

PLAY SELECTIVELY AGGRESSIVE

Most average or weak poker players who sometimes win, sometimes lose, in these medium and lower-limit games are passive players.

Most of the better players who win consistently in the medium and higher-limit games are aggressive players.

There is an obvious lesson for you in these two paragraphs. You can pick up extra bets and extra pots by playing aggressively. You'll win more often with your marginal hands. And as an aggressive player, you'll win more money with your good hands than a passive player holding the same hands.

Now before you go barging into every pot, putting in the maximum number of raises on every betting round with marginal hands, let me add a word: *selective*. I'm talking about being *selectively aggressive*.

A solid, skillful player might not play a lot of hands. But when he does play, he plays aggressively. He gets maximum value for the hand. He is selectively aggressive. You'll see what I mean as we go along.

Aggressive play is your best chance to win, in the short run or in the long run. Playing passively—consistently checking and calling, for example—just won't get the money. You're playing someone else's game. You've turned over the tempo and control of the game to your opponents.

Anytime you bet, you put the burden of deciding to call or fold onto your opponent. He might fold, giving you the win right there. But when you check and he bets, the burden is now on you.

You have given him the extra chance to win that would have been yours if you had bet instead of checked.

But again, a word of caution. Don't go off half-cocked, betting every hand, mindless of its value or the situation in which you find yourself. Stay with me as we progress down the path to poker money.

What makes the top players aggressive is the knowledge or talent to realize that aggressiveness is the way to win at poker. They didn't just sit down one day and say, "I think I'll be aggressive." They played enough poker to learn that playing aggressively is a successful way to play.

One of the world's top players told me, "When I sit down at the table, I want to have the other players' respect. I want to be in charge of that table. So they can expect a raise from me at any time. I want them to be aware that I'm in the game—to be looking to see what I'm going to do before they act, to be checking to me. Then I'm in control." But even here, the key is *selectively aggressive*.

This world-class player continued: "I might raise on fourth street in a seven-stud game with a four flush. Or maybe I don't actually *have* the four flush. I might have the six and seven of hearts showing, but two black deuces in the hole. If I put in a raise against a timid opponent and then buy a heart or an eight on the next card, there's a good chance my two deuces will win. Or I could buy an open pair or a deuce, and now I have a value hand."

Here's another example of being selectively aggressive: You start with 5-9-Q of spades. Your opponent starts with 5-9-Q of diamonds. The next two cards you catch are the four and five of clubs. Your opponent catches the four and five of hearts. You both started with the same hand, and you both broke off. So who wins the pot? The aggressive player will win the pot.

In the marginal situations, where both hands break off, the aggressive player will get in a bet that the passive player won't be willing to call.

That will amount to a fair amount of money for the aggressive player over the long run. But again, I stress being selectively aggressive.

Let's go back to a four-flush situation. Many times you'll see one of the better players checking a four flush. Not very aggressive, you say. But most likely, our better player is checking a relatively "dead" four flush. Let's say that he has four diamonds, with four other diamonds having shown on the board. He knows that he doesn't have a big opportunity to make the hand, so he doesn't push it.

But if no other diamonds have shown, he'll probably start pushing the hand, with a high probability of catching. The same would apply to a straight draw. Is it live or is it dead?

Most good players play aggressively with a hand that is already made, or a hand with good possibilities. But remember: selectively aggressive.

♠

COURSE LESSON 31

LOOSE OR TIGHT?

Here's a question often asked by my beginning students: "Should I play loose or should I play tight?" My answer is always, "Play solid."

Solid. I like the word. It sounds like strength. It has power and energy. It feels like a force unto itself. Vigor. Courage. Intensity. *Solid.*

Now look at and listen to the words "tight" and "loose." They sound almost sissified in comparison to "solid." So I'm certainly not going to recommend that my students play tight or loose.

Play solid! A solid player is a skillful player who sometimes plays tight and sometimes plays loose. He can be conservative or aggressive, depending on the situation. At the bottom line, a solid player roams the entire poker range from conservative to selectively aggressive. He has various strategies and knows when to use them.

A player who is only tight has little chance of scoring a big win, unless the cards run all over him. A player who is only loose has little chance of winning anything.

Correction—the loose player will win more pots than the solid player, but he'll put the money right back into the game. He'll win—but he won't take it home.

Play solid! Not many players do. The reason is that most of us are unwilling, or unable, to adapt from our basic life-styles. People generally don't make a conscious decision to play conservatively or to play aggressively. They tend to play one way or the other as a result of their basic natures. Most conservative players are conservative people. Most aggressive players are aggressive people. For one type to play like the other is to go against the grain. It's difficult—but it's not impossible. My students do it. *You* can do it.

If you play *consistently* conservative (tight) and I know that you will bet only when you are holding the nuts, why should I ever call one of your bets? You must show me a rag now and then to convince me that I have a chance of beating you. True, if you have a reputation of being consistently conservative, you can occasionally run a successful bluff. You *can*, but you probably won't. Conservative players aren't bluffers. It goes against the grain.

If you play *consistently* aggressive (loose) and I know you could be betting with anything, I'll be much more willing to call your bets while I'm holding marginal hands. From time to time in the natural course of events, you *will* be holding power and beat me. But not often enough to overcome all of the rags you've played. You'll give it back to me, or to another player. You won't take it home.

We can now see that the best course is an unpredictable course. It's called changing gears. It's called winning poker.

You'll need a conscious decision to change your style of play. The first several times, you'll feel strange and nervous. Proceed slowly. There's no need to set up an anxiety reaction. Experiment. Be comfortable with the change. Play *mostly* within your natural style.

Remember, you're not trying to change your style completely. You want to develop the ability to change *occasionally*—be able to comfortably change gears and keep your opponents guessing.

For the conservative player, loosening up a bit will make the game more interesting and exciting—and increase your win potential. For the rammer and jammer, slowing down will give you a chance to think about what you're doing—and increase your win potential.

You're welcome. ♠

COURSE LESSON 32

COSTLY MISTAKES YOU SHOULDN'T MAKE

That's an obvious but odd title for this Lesson. *Of course* we shouldn't make mistakes, costly or otherwise. But that's easier said than done. We don't realize it when we are making the mistake—otherwise, we wouldn't do it. (Or would we?)

So how do we keep from making mistakes if we don't notice ourselves making them? I'm glad you asked.

In my private poker lessons in Las Vegas, one of the assignments I give my students is to be constantly monitoring themselves for mistakes in their play. I now give you the same admonition: Before making any move at the poker table, ask yourself:

Is This A Mistake?

Train yourself—practice over and over—before taking any action at the table. Always ask yourself that question.

If what you are about to do isn't a mistake, then go ahead and do it. If you determine that it is a mistake, then don't do it. Simple.

However, if you realize that it *is* a mistake and then go ahead with the move *anyway*, with some rationalizing excuse for why you did it, then you'd better work on your discipline.

Example: You're holding a small four-flush at fourth street. You've seen four of your needed suit in other players' upcards. Too many. Then the voice in the back of your head says, "There are too many hearts out, but what the heck—I haven't played a hand in over twenty minutes. I'm gonna' go for it. Next time I'll be good." I doubt it. Next time it will be even easier to slip.

Stay disciplined. Train yourself until it becomes automatic to ask the question, *"Is this a mistake?"* This process will help you keep your discipline strong and intact. Your motivation is the knowledge that the consistent winners at poker are the players who make the fewest mistakes. Solid, mistake free poker is what gets the money at these low and medium limits. With all of this in mind, let's take a look at a few of the more common mistakes made by even regular, several-times-a-week players.

First of all, let's examine calling in very early position on third street when the only value to your hand is big overcards to the board. Generally, you want to play a hand like this from late position against one player. If you insist on playing it from an early position, *forget about calling.* You'll end up with too many opponents. You'd better raise to substantially narrow the field. Your best chance of winning is to eliminate the straight and flush draws and then pair up a big card, higher than any pair your opponent could be holding. That's essentially the only reason to play a hand that has only high cards as its value.

Another big mistake I've often seen players make is entering a pot at third street with a small pair and a low sidecard.

The only real improvement to such a hand is to make trips. You can't make two big pair because you have no high cards to pair.

The next mistake I've seen a lot of players make is to compound the above error by continuing to play when they pair that small sidecard. Fives and threes just isn't much of a poker hand at these limits. About the only hand they'll beat is one pair.

So many mistakes. Next one: Playing when your cards are not live. If you've come this far through this Course, you probably have a full appreciation of the value of a hand with live cards as opposed to the same hand without live cards. Just as hold'em is a game of big cards, seven-card stud is a game of live cards. If you get nothing else from this Course, *get that.*

Okay, what's next on the mistake list? Not stealing the antes at every opportunity. In any game with an ante, if you're not stealing, you're falling behind. *See Lesson 15 on ante-stealing.*

Next: Checking dark on the end when you are on a flush draw. Players who check on seventh street without looking at their last card ("check dark") do so mostly to stop someone else from betting. The implied threat is, "I check before looking to see if I have made my hand, so if you bet I might raise so watch out." The problem is, you are acting without information. You might intimidate an opponent into checking along; then you look at your last card and see that you have made your hand. You missed a bet. Also, if a strong opponent makes any kind of a hand he's going to bet despite your implied threat. That puts the "threat" back onto you, and now you must decide whether he bet because he made a winning hand or because you have shown weakness.

More? Okay: Letting your ego into the game. I've seen it a hundred times in public poker. One player will raise another player's bet on an early street, not because of the value of his hand, but because he doesn't like his opponent. "Raise me? Well, I raise *you*, wise guy." The initial bettor's ego isn't going to stand for that. "Oh yeah? Well, back at you, buddy." So we have these two players warring, with neither of them strong enough to have stood the first raise. As I watch, I know that in about a minute and a half, one of these guys is going to be kicking himself in the butt for ever having gotten involved in the hand. The other will be congratulating himself for his brilliant playing.

Ego tells every poker player in the world that his wins are because of his superior skill, while his losses are just bad luck. Most players believe it. I do, don't you?

Another way your ego can do you dirty is to keep you playing in the game you'd like to beat instead of the game you can beat.

Don't let your ego move you up to the higher

limits too soon, before you're ready with an adequate bankroll, experience, and a lot of heart.

Here's another common error that I used to occasionally commit out of frustration—until I saw that it costs me money. Some days you just can't seem to pick up a starting hand, and to make matters worse, you keep getting hit with the low card at third street. The mistake is tossing in your forced bet *and* your garbage hand along with it. The problem is that you might have paired one of your cards on fourth street, for instance, seen everyone check, then tripped up on fifth street, and made a full house at sixth street. Admittedly that's a stretch, but I've seen such things happen.

Chasing—and not chasing—are two more mistakes. In every pot, one player has the best hand and everyone else is chasing. You are chasing whenever you are playing without the best hand, trying to outdraw your opponents. (It's also called "going uphill."

Any time you are drawing to a straight or a flush you are, by definition, chasing any player who has a pair. You are justified in your chase if your drawing hand has live overcards to your opponent's probably pair. If you don't make the hand you're drawing to, you can still beat him by pairing one of your overcards and going on to make two pair or trips.

Chase only when the pot is giving you the proper odds for the hand you are trying to make. If you regularly chase with 5-to-1 hands when you are getting only 3-to-1 pot odds, for example, you will be a long-range money loser. And of course you'll want to consider this question: "If I make the hand I am drawing to, is it likely that I will win the pot?"

You can chase with a smaller pair than your opponent's pair if yours is hidden and live, and if your sidecard (which is also live) is an overcard to your opponent's probable pair.

One more: This mistake is not calling at seventh street without your knowing for certain that the bettor has you beaten. If you have any reasonable chance of winning the pot, even with only a fair hand, it usually is best to call for that one last bet on seventh street. If he has you beat, you lose one more bet. But if you throw away the best hand, you lose a whole pot.

I repeat my earlier admonition: Constantly monitor yourself for mistakes in your game. Keep asking yourself, "Is this a mistake?" ♠

COURSE LESSON 33

THE FUEL OF POKER

The fuel of poker is money. No money, no poker. Ever play poker without money? The game quickly falls apart because nothing is at risk. Everyone bets the universe at every card. No value, no risk. No risk, no game. It's as simple as that. So you need money to play poker.

So let's talk about your bankroll. What is it? Why do you need one? Where do you get it?

All medium and lower-limit poker players eventually experience a time in their playing careers when they ponder moving up to play a higher limit. The smaller games are offering small, consistent wins. It follows then that a larger game would offer *larger* consistent wins. And wouldn't that be nice. But before you move up—think.

Your most important thoughts should be about your bankroll. Is it big enough for the limit you want to play? And how big is big enough?

Most medium and low-limit players never consider the question of bankroll. They usually just sit down and play with the money they happen to have in their jeans. If it's enough for a buy-in, they play. If it's not, they don't. Their "bankroll"

162

is whatever cash they happen to be holding at the time. For many of these players, a loss breaks them and they can't play again until they acquire more money, probably by waiting until payday.

For the most part, medium and low-limit players are recreational players who sometimes win, sometimes lose. Mostly, they manage to stay about even or run a little behind—nothing really serious or they couldn't keep playing. But they all eventually look across the room to a higher-limit game and think about walking over there to have a seat. This thought usually occurs to them when they're scored a nice win.

It's just a short walk from over here to over there. But keep in mind, it's a *long* walk back. When *you* go over there, plan ahead, so you'll be able to *stay* over there.

A bankroll. What is it? A bankroll is *not* the money you happen to have on you at the moment. A bankroll is a specific amount of money you have set aside for the purpose of playing the game of poker.

Your rent does not come out of your bankroll. Neither does gasoline, shoes, or trolley fare. Your bankroll is playing money. Period.

Why do you need a bankroll? If you're playing with whatever money you happen to have with you, the first loss will send you right back to the lower limit, or even out of action entirely. *So you have to be prepared for a loss.* That's why you need a bankroll.

Your bankroll is "where you go" to get back into action. If you're not in action you can't win. And if you don't have a bankroll, you can't be in action.

How much money should you have in your bankroll? As much as you can muster. The more you have in reserve, the more comfortable you'll feel about playing at the higher limit. And if you're not comfortable, it's going to be difficult to win.

Feel at ease when you sit down so that you could, if need be, afford some short-term reverses.

Don't play on a short bankroll, especially when you're moving up to a higher limit. It's too tough psychologically.

If you take a few losses, you could be devastated. Be comfortable.

Consider these amounts as minimums for playing regularly at the indicated limits. To play $1-$4 or $1-$5, you'll want a bankroll of *at least* $1,500 devoted exclusively to playing poker. At $3-$6, $2,000. To play regularly in the $5-$10 limit games, sock away $3,000 before you sit down. At $10-$20, you'll want $6,000. I want to stress again that there are *minimums*—and this money is for playing poker *only*.

Where do you get this bankroll? The absolute best way to acquire it would be to save it out of your winnings from the lower-limit games. There's nothing like playing on someone else's money.

So here's an incentive to increase your poker skills and sharpen your play. Your wins are going toward a bankroll so that you can move up in limits and build an even bigger bankroll and then move up again.

Large luck! ♠

COURSE LESSON 34

How Much?

Student poker players often ask how much they should lose before quitting a given game. And how much to win. I have no formulas or set amounts, but I do have some thoughts.

As for how much to lose—poker authorities used to give percentages and amounts and formulas to set limits on your losses. But I make it much simpler than that. Now I say:

Quit when it begins to hurt.

The amount is completely subjective. For one person it might "hurt" at $20. For another it might be $20,000. The number isn't important. What is important is the effect it has on you and your playing ability.

If you're hurting, either financially or emotionally, you won't be playing your best poker.

Consider too that when you are losing it's possible that your game is off somewhere. Maybe you took a bad beat and it has affected your play without your even realizing it. (It happens, even to the pros.) You might have become a bit less aggressive after getting a couple of hands cracked, so you don't make the raise where you normally would. Maybe you're just being outplayed. Or maybe your game is right on, in top form, but your cards just aren't holding up.

If you are losing, something is wrong somewhere. Unless you can discover what that something is, I think you'll be better off getting up and absorbing the loss. Tomorrow is another day—hopefully a better day.

As for how much to win, no more formulas here either—and no limits. If you're winning, and are favored to keep winning, keep playing. I personally like to play from four to six hours in a session, and make my decision about staying or leaving during the last two hours. But if the people I'm playing with are having a party and giving away money, I'll stay as long as the party lasts and I'm getting the most favors.

Most professional players don't let their winning or losing be the deciding factor in whether they play or leave.

Rather, they make their judgment on the basis of whether the game is potentially a good money maker, or a dull, grind-it-out affair.

So it appears that the only reason for leaving a good game, other than discovering that you are not up to playing your best, is one of personal considerations. You may be tired, or hungry, or have a commitment elsewhere.

Remember the old saying: "If it's raining money, turn your umbrella upside down." ♠

COURSE LESSON 35

LOSING IS MEANINGLESS: IT JUST DOESN'T MATTER

Has Mr. West gone mad? Care he not for the rewards of skillful poker? The transfer of monies from unskilled players to those of skill? What does he mean: *losing is meaningless and it just doesn't matter?*

Winning is not usually a problem for a poker player. But losing can be. You don't have to *cope* with winning, but you do have to cope with losing. So let's consider losing.

It's meaningless. It just doesn't matter.

Consider that you will play in only one poker game during your entire lifetime. The game of poker was being played for many years before you were born, and it will continue long after you are gone. The game is always being played, somewhere. We can consider, then, that in terms of your lifetime, poker is a continuous game with no beginning and no end. There is no conclusion. Therefore, being ahead or behind for a certain session is of *no real importance.*

Poker is not like baseball where, when the game is completely over, there is a winner and a loser. Poker is more like comparing the third inning to the fourth inning. Or, as another example, it is like going for the pennant. In that case, you have to play something like 162 games. So if you win or lose the first few game of the season, it's not conclusive. You still have 155 games to go. You don't have to win all 162 games. If you win somewhere around 100, you'll be in the playoffs.

So your play is not based on winning every day, but on winning in the long run.

With that in mind, you won't consider a loss on a given day to be important. You'll be back tomorrow to continue winning. ♠

COURSE LESSON 36

"How Much Money Can I Make Playing Poker?"

Actually, there is no top—and there is no bottom. Many players have made over a million dollars playing poker. Many have gone broke in the attempt. Most of us are somewhere between.

A general rule of thumb bandied about in the poker business says that a solid player (*you*, when you finish this Course) will win an amount equal to about one bet per hour of the upper limit of your regular game. At $5-$10 you should be winning $10 per hour as an average over a year's time. At $10-$20 it would be more like $20 per hour

Rarely will you make exactly that amount in a day's play. Most days you'll win. Some days you'll lose. But when you average it out over a period of months or a year, it should come out close.

And that's a good reason to keep records. If you don't, how can you tell (outside of a guess) if you are winning or losing, and by how much? And if you're losing, why? But if you don't even know you're losing, you can't do anything about it. ♠

COURSE LESSON 37

SEVERAL WAYS

Often there is more than one "correct" way to play the same hand. There are variations in situations—variations in opponents. You might play the same hand differently because you have specific knowledge of this specific opponent. "There is *no* substitute for knowledge of your opponents."

What I've done in this Course is give you *preferred* ways—and some alternatives. It's not possible to cover every situation in this Course (or in any book), but the examples I've given will enable you to figure the best action to take in situations that I have not specifically covered. ♠

COURSE LESSON 38

QUESTIONS FOR THE INSIDE OF YOUR HEAD

Decisions at the poker table are based on information. You get most of this information by closely observing your opponents, and by asking questions of yourself. With practice and concentration, you can ask—and answer—these and other questions in a matter of a few seconds:

What's my objective? That question should always be rattling around inside your head while you're playing poker. If you don't know where you're going, you might end up somewhere else.

By *objective,* I don't mean "to win money today," or "to have a good time," or "to have stories to tell back home." By *objective,* I mean what you are trying to accomplish right now with these cards you're holding at this moment against these players and the cards they are holding in this hand. (Wow, there's a mouthful!) The next question accompanies this one.

How can I best accomplish this objective? That, of course, depends on the objective. But be aware that sometimes you can't accomplish your objective. Example: We've already learned in this Course that, generally, your objective with a big pair such as kings at third street is to play the hand against one player with a smaller pair, and possibly one other player on a drawing hand. You accomplish that objective by raising at third street. But wait a minute: Suppose the forced-bet low card is immediately to your left. He opens. Five other players call before the action gets to you. Your raise at that point would probably drop the low card and one other player only. At these limits, once many of these players have some money in the pot, you can't get them out with a cannon.

So you'll still have to play the hand against too many players. Consider calling and hoping for the best. Of course, "hoping for the best" is not a great poker strategy. But sometimes that's all you can do.

Now let's look at the other side of that problem. This time, let's say that the forced-bet low card is immediately to your *right*. Now you're going to act right under the gun and so you have a chance to put in a raise and drop most of your opponents. Not having already invested in the pot, your opponents are much less likely to come in. Of course you're not going to knock out any big hands, but you'll probably get rid of the drawing hands and the small pairs that might have stuck around to trip up and beat you. Objective accomplished.

What's my position? You should know your position at all times without having to stop and think about it. Knowing your position should have a top priority in your mind.

If they play long enough, most players will figure out that it's best to be the last to act—after the other players have already acted by checking, betting, raising, etc. This is usually the first insight about position that new players come to understand.

In a poker game, position is simply a matter of how many players will be able to act after you do. You must consider what those players might do *before* you decide what you are going to do. If you are first to act, you have to make your best evaluation about what the players behind you will do.

If you are holding only a fair hand, you won't want to bet it into several hands yet to act. If one of them raises, you're going to be either trapped for two bets if you call, or surrender one bet if you decide to fold.

If you hold that same fair hand in *last* position, you'll already know what action the other players have taken by the time it is your turn to act. Now you have much more information on which to base a decision.

While position is important, it will affect your play the most when you hold a "fair to middling" hand. When your hand is strong, you'll usually have to bet it no matter what your position—unless it's so strong that you decide to slow play it or go for a check raise. Even then, you want to be aware of your position. How many players are left to act behind you? What will be their likely response to your action? How can you coax the most money from your hand? (Notice how position figures into the question, "What's my objective?")

More questions that figure into position: How many players are already in the pot? What action have they taken? How many can still come in? What do I know about what they might do if I check or bet or call or raise? And this last question ties back into the premise that there is no substitute for knowledge of your opponents. (*See Lesson 2, "Poker Is A People Game."*)

What are my opponents showing on their boards? The only way you know for sure what cards are out-of-play or unavailable to you is to see them appear on the board, beginning right from third street. If you don't pay attention to them, you could end up drawing dead, having missed seeing that most of the cards you need to fill your straight are already gone. (*See Lesson 3, "Remembering Exposed Cards."*)

If I make the hand I'm drawing to, is it likely to be a winner? You won't want to find yourself drawing to a straight when three other players appear to be drawing to flushes. Even if you make the hand, you are probably going to lose. Same with small flushes drawing against big flushes. Same with any flush when two opponents have each made open pairs and have started a raising war; one or both probably has made a full house.

Do I want my opponents in or out? It depends on what hand I'm trying to make and what I perceive my opponents trying to make. If you have a big pair at third street, you want most of your opponents out so that your chances of winning without improvement will be increased. But if you start at third street with a drawing hand, you want opponents in to give you the proper pot odds to draw to the hand.

7 CARD STUD

How big is the pot? You'll want to keep track of the pot in a general manner: You don't need to know exactly how much is in it—an estimate will do. If the pot size is $37.50, a general figure of $40.00 will do. Why? Read on.

Here are three questions in one: What are the odds against making this hand; what are the pot odds; and am I then justified in drawing to this hand?

Pot odds and drawing odds, and their relationship to one another, is a mystery to many medium and low-limit players. Let me simplify it for you. Elsewhere in this Course, you will find a list telling you what the odds are against making any particular hand. You should know that much, at a minimum. Now, what are the pot odds? To again simplify, let's say there is $40 in the pot. Your opponent bets $10. Now with $50 in the pot, if you want to call the bet you have to put in $10. The pot is giving you 5-to-1 odds. If the hand you are trying for is less than 5-to-1, mathematically you have a good bet. But this doesn't mean that you will win the pot. These are just the odds against making the hand. You might make the hand and still lose the pot.

Now let's say that you have a hand that is 5-to-1 against making and there is $20 in the pot. Your opponent bets $10. The pot is giving you 3-to-1 odds. You don't have a good bet.

By the way, pot odds and drawing odds are the reasons you "never draw to an inside straight." Everyone in America knows that, they learned it from the movies. But they don't know the reason. It is because an inside-straight draw is usually about 12- or 13-to-1 against making. And usually, the pot won't be offering you these odds. Now if the pot would give you 18-to-1 odds, you could draw to inside straights all day and make money.

Without information you're not making decisions—you are guessing. You don't want to make guesses—you want to make decisions, which are based on information, which you get by asking these questions. ♠

Seven-Card Stud Tournament Tactics

by Tom McEvoy,
1983 World Champion of Poker &
author of "Championship Tournament Poker"

Introduction

Seven-card stud is one of the most demanding tournament games you can play. The strategies you use to win in regular games don't always work in tournaments, so you have to make some changes in your game plan. In these Lessons, I will outline some plays that will help you wind up in the winner's circle.

Your strategy in each phase of a tournament is

influenced by four major factors: the size of your stack compared to your opponents' stacks; the stage of the tournament (early, middle, late, or final table); your position in the hand (first to act, last to act, etc.); and how much time is left in the round.

For example, you might play a somewhat weaker starting hand more aggressively if you have a tall stack in the late stage and will be competing against only one opponent whose stack is short, especially if the antes will be increasing on the next round and if your board indicates that you will be last to act. However, if you have a big hand very late in the tournament against an aggressive opponent who raises your opening bet *and* has a stack of chips that is equal to or greater than yours, you will most likely fold because tournament strategy suggests that you avoid big confrontations in the late stages.

COURSE LESSON 39

EARLY STAGE

Generally speaking, players in the early rounds of seven-card stud tournaments play more conservatively than they do in their regular games. They usually wait more patiently for a good starting hand and play cautiously on each street. Although this is not always true, you can easily recognize opponents who are not following this policy because they call more opening bets to see fourth street, and they raise more often than their hands seem to warrant.

If most of your opponents are playing very tight, you can play somewhat more loosely and try to steal a few more antes. You will want to play a very solid game, although a bit looser than your tighter opponents. Conversely, if your adversaries are playing looser than ordinary, you should play a little tighter than they do. As Roy has already suggested, *solid aggressive* is your best approach.

The earlier a player raises, the more credit you should give him for having a good hand. The majority of the time when a player raises with a pair, that pair will be the same as his doorcard. But when an early-position player raises with a small card (such as a 4) showing, be cautious because he probably has a big hidden pair (tens or higher).

Playing flushes. Suppose a player raises from an early position and you hold a three-flush. For you to call, you need to have a rather large flush draw with no more than one or two of your suit showing on the board, and it would be even better to have one or two cards higher than the raiser's doorcard. So if you are fairly sure that you'll be playing against a big pair, you should be drawing to hands that are both live and contain one or two overcards.

Be leery of playing small three-flushes in raised pots. If you can play for the minimum bet and your hand is live, you can see fourth street. When I am in late position with a small flush draw and hold higher cards than the forced bring-in bet, I may even raise. But I will only do this when five people have passed and only one other player (in addition to the forced bring-in bettor) is left to act—and his upcard must be lower than mine because then he is less likely to reraise.

If you play your flush draw past third street in these early stages, keep a close count of how many of your suit cards are exposed. If you improve by catching another suited card on fourth street, you have close to an even-money chance of completing your flush (depending on how many of your suit cards are out). Therefore, it is usually correct to continue playing the hand because the pot will often be paying a good enough price.

Of course, you don't necessarily have a through ticket to the river with a four-flush. Other players may also be catching suited cards higher than yours, and someone may pair his doorcard, both of which are threats to your flush draw. Most of the time, a player who pairs his doorcard has made trips if he started with a pair. Few things are more devastating than completing your flush only to be beaten by a full house.

Suppose you have four cards to a flush on fourth street and your opponent bets into you. Raise, especially if two additional players sitting in front of you have called the original bettor. Good players will probably read you for a flush draw, but that's okay because you still have a 45-50 percent chance of making your hand, depending on how many of your suit are showing.

The object of raising with your four flush is to get a free card on fifth street when the bets double and your opponents check to you, which is what you hope they will do. Of course, if you improve to a pair that appears to be higher than your opponents, you can value bet instead of taking the free card because you have both a flush draw and a pair working.

This play works much better if your opponent has a king or queen showing on fourth street because unless you pair up or spike an ace, he will remain the first to act with his high board. You must consider this factor before you decide whether to raise on fourth street. Of course, if your opponent is a very aggressive player and is likely to reraise, you aren't going to get the free fifth-street card your raise was intended to receive. In this case, you are better off just calling. The bottom line is a concept that Roy has hammered home in this book: You must have a good *read* on your adversary to determine whether a fourth street raise will work to your advantage.

Another time that you won't want to raise is when two or more players are left to act behind you, because your raise may cause them to fold. In this case, you are better off to just call because you want to have as many people in the pot as possible when you are drawing to a flush to improve your pot odds, and so that you can make as much money as possible if you make your flush.

However, raising when they are sitting between you and the first bettor is a different story because they have already committed one bet to the pot. If the original bettor decides to reraise and they all fold, you have their dead money in the pot with the same chance of making your hand. So you aren't in bad shape, no matter what you do. Furthermore, if you do make you hand, there often will be enough confusion in your opponents' minds for them to pay you off.

Creating confusion. Creating confusion is a valuable poker skill. When your opponents are not able to put you on a proper hand, they often will call you with any type of reasonable hand. So if you are able to disguise the strength of your hand, you will get a lot of calls just because *your opponents are confused* about what you are probably holding.

When you put in a raise with two suited cards showing against *intelligent* opponents, they will put you on a probable four-flush, especially when their doorcards are higher than either of your two upcards. But even though your raise may tip them off to your flush draw, they still may be forced to continue playing with a reasonable hand because they are not sure *exactly* what you have. This tiny bit of confusion on their part can add extra bets to your win when you make your hand.

Playing Straights. Straight draws are the most overrated starting hands in seven-card stud: They often create more problems than they are worth. On the rare occasions in a tournament when you are playing in a multi-way pot against four or five people, you can reasonably assume that two or three of them are drawing to a flush. Straight draws do not play well against flush draws.

Therefore, if your opponents show any improvement on fourth street with either a suited card or a suited connector (which could enable them to make either a straight or a flush), you must play a straight draw with extreme caution—and it cannot be played at all against a raiser who holds a doorcard higher than any of your three straight cards.

As a general rule, fold your straight draws early and often unless they are very live. If you decide to draw to your straight, be very leery of a raiser who may have a high pair. You're better off passing. You can feel somewhat more comfortable, of course, if all three of your straight cards are higher than his doorcard.

Suppose you enter an unraised pot with three to a straight, or you have cards higher than the raiser's doorcard in a raised pot. You have improved your hand on fourth street by either pairing, or by catching a fourth card to your straight (with a hand such as 9-10-J, for example, you catch a 7 and don't see any 8s on the board). Under these conditions, you can continue playing until fifth street. Of course, if you spot one or two 8s showing on fifth street and an opponent bets into you, you must pass, *unless* you also have a pair. Even if your pair doesn't appear to be the best one, you probably still have enough outs (even with an inside straight draw) to continue playing the hand. But you need all four of your straight cards to be live if you continue playing with an inferior pair. Try to play the hand as cheaply as possible; if you can get a free card, take it. And if you think your pair has become the best hand on fifth street, value bet based on its strength.

Sometimes, a hand as strong as A-K-Q is playable, even for a raise or possibly a reraise, unless the reraise comes from an ace or king showing. In that case, you simply must pass. Say a 9 has brought in the pot for a raise and a queen has reraised. You hold A-K-Q and suspect the reraiser may have queens. If there are no aces, kings, jacks or 10s showing (or one, at the most), you are justified in taking off a card with your two overcards. With three overcards to the raiser's doorcard, and if he really has the hand he is representing, you still have a very close hand. But if the raise or reraise comes from a player with an ace or king and you are fairly certain he has either aces or kings, you should pass even if no jacks or 10s are showing.

When you make a pair on fourth street (along with your straight draw) but see no apparent improvement to your opponent's hand, you can continue value betting, even if you are reasonably sure your opponent has overcards. So long as you think you have the best pair, even though your opponent has overcards (but has not caught a threatening-looking card such as a suited connector), you can continue value betting until you have reason to believe you are beaten.

If you started with three overcards and your hand is live, you can probably justify taking off a card on fourth street if you don't seem to be in danger of being raised by an opponent behind you. But if you are in danger of being raised, you can't call that first bet on fourth street and will have to pass. If you are heads up and have not improved by fifth street, you will have to give it up if your opponent continues betting.

If you have four to a straight on fourth street, your chances of making your hand are not quite as good as they would be if you had a four-flush. But with a reasonable hand, enough money in the pot, and overcards, you have adequate reason to play to the river, unless you think someone has either filled up, or has paired his doorcard with a strong potential to fill up, or has made a flush.

Be very leery when you are playing straight draws against flush draws in multiway pots. In tournaments, however, you often have only one or two active opponents in most pots, so you are usually getting enough incentive from the pot odds and your live hand to continue playing to the river.

7 CARD STUD

What you are looking for in seven-card stud is either the best *starting* hand, which is usually the highest pair, or the best *drawing* hand, which is either three big straight cards or a three-flush with overcards to the raiser's doorcard. You want either one or the other: the best starting hand or the best drawing hand.

I caution tournament players, however, to remember this: Playing too many drawing hands in tourneys is usually a mistake. I exact multiple criteria for my drawing hands, one of which is the possession of overcards so that, if I don't improve to the flush possibility I started with, at least I have a chance of making the best hand with a higher pair than my opponents.

Playing Pairs. Most stud players do a lot of raising on third street to try to force out weaker pairs and marginal drawing hands. The reason is obvious: When you start with the best pair, you have a much better chance of winning *without improvement* if you are against only one or two opponents. What you hope to do is isolate and eliminate players so that you can play heads up with your big pair. Although it isn't always possible to accomplish this, you can at least punish people for trying to draw out on you by making them put in extra money.

Sometimes your opponents will draw out on you because they don't put you on the correct hand, or because they think you are either bluffing or semi-bluffing. Or they may have a good pair themselves or a live overcard to your doorcard.

If you think you may have the worst pair, only one overcard makes any sense in prompting you to continue with the hand: *an ace.* If you have the ace overcard, it is better to have it buried because of its deceptive value if you catch another ace.

Playing Pair Against Pair. Suppose you begin with what you think is the best starting pair and your opponent catches up with you when he makes an open pair (but one that does not pair his doorcard).

For example, say you raised with a 9 and have been called by a player with an 8. On fourth street, he catches a 6 while you catch a random jack that doesn't help you. On fifth street, your opponent draws another 6 and you catch a deuce. You believe he now holds 8s and 6s. What should you do against your opponent's probable two pair? So long as you are sure your opponent has made no better than 8s and 6s, you can continue playing. You are hoping to make either a second pair or trips, which will give you the winning hand provided your opponent gets no further help.

Of course, you can no longer play aggressively. You have to take a more defensive posture by just calling. If your opponent bets into you on the river, you would have a tough call with only one pair because the only hand you could beat would be a busted draw and the one open pair he's betting. In this case, it is correct to fold on the river unless you have a very good read on your opponent as having only the one pair with a busted flush or straight draw. But that would be a risky call which you wouldn't want to make very often.

Now suppose you have made two pair and your opponent bets into you on the river. Normally, you should just call because you can't be certain he hasn't made either trips or is holding a big pocket pair such as aces or kings which he has been value betting. Of course, against an aggressive player whom you think is capable of betting 8s and 6s, you should consider a raise, which can be a very close judgment call.

Playing Rolled-Up Trips. This is a hand that will win you a lot of money when you are fortunate enough to get it, but it can also be very expensive when you lose with it. The following tips will help you to maximize your chances of winning with rolled-up trips.

First of all, remember that in tournaments, you are not usually trying to get full value from each good starting hand, as you would be trying to do in a side game. Survival is more important than squeezing an extra bet from your premium hands. It is better to win a smaller pot than it is to risk getting drawn out on in a large pot.

This concept is more important in the later stages than in the early stages of tournaments, when you still have enough time and chips to recover when you suffer a bad beat. So in the early stage, you can gamble a little bit more with rolled-up trips than you can later on.

With small trips such as deuces, treys, fours or fives, if the pot is shaping up as a multiway contest, you will be in greater jeopardy of being drawn out on than you would be in a two or three-way pot. Therefore, if you have limped in with your small trips, which is usually the correct thing to do, you may want to raise or check-raise on fourth or fifth street in an attempt to limit the field.

Base your strategy on your betting objectives. If your objective is to eliminate players from a multi-way pot, you probably will have to raise to achieve that goal. Based on your evaluation of your opponents, play rolled-up trips with the strategy you think will get the most money into the pot. If you think slow playing on fourth street and then raising on fifth street will do it, play that strategy. Or if you think it would it be best to wait until sixth street, then, fine—do that. ♠

COURSE LESSON 40

MIDDLE STAGE

Your stack size relative to that of your opponents becomes an important factor in the middle stages. Be more willing to gamble against short stacks that have only enough chips for one or two more bets. With small to medium pairs, be more willing to gamble against a short stack. What you want to avoid is giving action to a small stack when a *third* player is involved in the hand, especially if he is sitting behind you with a threatening-looking card and could raise, in which case you might be holding the third-best hand. So be reasonably certain you will be heads up against a short stack before you do battle with him.

Heads up against a short stack, I will give some loose action with the worst pair. It won't hurt me very much and I have a reasonable chance of drawing out against him. I am inclined to gamble with hands such as three-straights or small three-flushes that I might fold in other circumstances.

Be careful about the types of drawing hands you play in these middle stages—even more careful than you were in the early stages when it didn't cost you as much if you failed to make your draw. You may have to expend one third or more of your stack to play a drawing hand in the middle stage, and you want to avoid doing that if you possibly can. *Be very selective with drawing hands in tournaments.*

With a large to medium stack, use a solid approach to every hand. Prefer to play more on the side of caution, except against a very tight, passive opponent. Then you can try to capitalize on his tight play by playing somewhat more liberally, perhaps putting in a raise with a medium pair, semi-bluffing, or trying an occasional ante-steal.

But when you have a short stack and are up against a tall stack, you cannot afford to jeopardize yourself with a weak drawing hand. You must wait for something better. Short stacks are more likely to get called by tall stacks because it won't cost them very much to try to eliminate a player. So if you're the short stack, use your best judgment about when to commit your chips. Naturally, you would rather commit with a split pair and an ace kicker than you would with a small three-flush. Your chances of either having the best hand at the start or of improving to the best hand with your ace kicker are much better than you would have with your three-flush or three-straight.

Don't lose patience when you have a short stack in the middle rounds. Pick your spot—usually, with three high cards or a good pair. If you have only enough for one or two bets, it is probably better to be aggressive early with your pair and simply go all in. But if you have been forced to play a drawing hand with only enough chips left for two or three bets, you may not want to fully commit on third street. If you don't improve on fourth street, you can still escape with enough chips for a few more antes, a few more opportunities to make a comeback.

With a medium or large stack, try to avoid playing small pairs against other medium to large stacks. But if you have such a short stack that you think your pair may be the best hand you're going to get, then play it. Most of the time, abandon small pairs unless it will cost you only one or two bets and will put you heads up against a short stack.

In tournaments, it is often correct to put in a bet with a negative expectation. For example, when you have a hand that may not be the favorite to win, but it will win just often enough to make it correct for you to play against a short stack. With a little luck, you may be able to draw out on him at minimal expense. It is important to put players all-in at every opportunity in the middle stages because even with a short stack, they can make inroads quickly.

Be wary, however, about giving too much action with a truly terrible hand. For example, if you made the forced bet with a deuce showing and have 3-7 in the hole, it isn't worth it to call an all-in bettor who raises with a 5 showing. But if your cards were 4-5-6, for example, you would have a reasonable chance to improve and may consider making the call. Another type of hand with which you might call one extra bet against the short stack is A-K in the hole, because you have two overcards and you could outdraw him if you get lucky.

You *allow yourself to get lucky* by solid play that enables you to survive and accumulate enough chips so that you can take a few gambles such as this in select situations. It is your good, solid play in other stages of the tournament that has set the stage for you to get lucky when you think it is necessary to occasionally take the worst of it. ♠

COURSE LESSON 41

LATE STAGE

You will need to raise far more often than you call in the later stages of a tournament. You should be trying to take the lead yourself, or isolate the action heads-up with one other player. With judicious raising and a good sense of timing, you can also pick up some additional antes.

Taking advantage of tight play in the late stage is crucial. It gives you the chance to jockey yourself into position to make the last table with a reasonable number of chips. The antes are usually quite high, making it worth the extra risk to pick up a few pots against tight players. However, you must also be ready to put on the brakes.

Ante Stealing. Suppose you have a king showing with A-8 in the hole. Your king is the highest upcard and all your cards are live. Only one or two other players are yet to act. You try an ante-steal and get called by a player with a 4 showing. What should you do on fourth street when your opponent catches what appears to be a bad card (in this example, a 9) and you catch a scary-looking card such as a jack or 10 (which doesn't really help you)? Fire a bet with your two high upcards in hopes of picking up the pot.

If he again calls with a raggedy front like 9-4, you are faced with a judgment decision as to what to do on fifth street. If you catch another scare card such as a queen (giving you an inside straight draw), and he catches a random 7, for example, go ahead and make another bet. If he calls you this time—or worse yet, if he raises—you must seriously evaluate your next move. If he raises, you are in a very bad situation with only an inside straight draw against a hand that probably has a minimum of one big pair and possibly two pair or even trips. Your opponent would have to be very brave to put in a total bluff on fifth street with his ragged-looking board cards against your strong front.

Now suppose your adversary catches a suited connector to his doorcard on fifth street, for example, and you catch a bad card like a deuce or trey. You must check to him, hope for a free card, and just pass if he bets. In this situation, it makes no sense to continue representing strength you don't have.

Seven-card stud is a game of strong-looking boards. Be reluctant to continue playing against such a board in the late stages, and especially against several opponents. You would need a very strong hand yourself to continue. Therefore, even if you suspect a player is on a bluff or semi-bluff, if he catches two powerful looking face cards to go with the unmatched one he already has, you're taking too much of a risk to continue playing hands such as medium pairs, for example.

You can't afford to be a *sheriff* in a tournament, trying to keep the other players honest. The best players in the world get bluffed more often than weaker players because they are more capable of making a big laydown. So in the late stages, you can capitalize on the play of a conservative player who will make a laydown when he believes you have him beaten. However, if you see that your opponents are willing to defend with medium-strength hands, your hand must be at least as good as the one they are defending with before you begin splashing around too often. ♠

ROY WEST · CARDOZA PUBLISHING

COURSE LESSON 42

THE FINAL TABLE

If you have arrived at the final table with a short or medium stack against several tall stacks, you will need to put your patience to the test by waiting for the best situation possible to put in your money. If your back is to the wall and you're down to only one or two bets, you will probably need to throw them in on a medium pair, three big cards, or a strong looking three-flush that is fairly live.

In very few seven-card stud tourneys do you ever ante yourself broke. The antes are usually small enough in relation to future bets that you can wait for a premium hand. But once you decide to make your final commitment with a short stack, put the heat on as early as possible. You hope to either eliminate players or to make your opponents put in their money early so that if you end up with the best hand, you can get full value from the pot. With a short stack, it is a bad play to put in only the minimum bet when you know you will need to go all-in on a later street, no matter what your opponents do. Also, if you just call, the opponents left to act behind you can get away from their hands on fourth street, for example, without putting in any extra chips.

When the table is down to either three players or you are heads-up against only one opponent, you will have to do far more ante stealing than you have

199

previously done. You must also be prepared to put on the brakes more quickly because your opponents won't continue to let you bully them without taking a stand. So if you get caught in a bluff or semi-bluff, be prepared to muck your hand quickly.

If you are on a semi-bluff and get called, whether you fold on fourth street depends upon your style of play. If you are on a three-flush, for example, catch nothing at all on fourth street, and don't have a frightening front, you are better off to pass, even if your opponent's front also looks weak. If he called you on third street with a small pair, for example, give it up if you can't even beat that.

On the other hand, if you are semi-bluffing and catch a card that pairs you or gives you either a four-flush or a four-straight, you can continue to play the hand so long as you have overcards. You may continue betting into your opponent, if you are first to act.

If you're against a very aggressive player, be selective about when you take a stand. If he seems willing to mix it up with you, you may try a reraise bluff or semi-bluff, although they are very risky moves. But if it looks as though nothing will slow him down, you should wait and try to pick him off with better cards.

Heads-up play requires a fairly accurate evaluation of your opponent. By this stage of the tournament, you should be able to read him rather well: his style, what's going through his mind, and so on. Remember that it takes far less strength to get involved in a pot heads-up than it does when even as few as three or four players are left.

"Raise and take it" will probably become the order of the day with the high upcard raising the smaller one. Suppose the low upcard is a deuce and you have a jack showing. You probably have a far greater chance of taking the pot with a raise than you would if the low card were an 8 and you held a 9. When you have nothing at all, you are better off just passing.

There are two occasions when you can limp in heads-up rather than raise. One is with a marginal hand such as a 9 up against an 8. If you have 7-10 in the hole, for example, you may want to take off a card. Although you are looking for that perfect 8, you might also catch one of your overcards and end up with the best pair. Another time you may want to flat-call with such a marginal hand is when you hold a three-flush and only your upcard is higher than your opponent's doorcard. You hope to either pair your high card or catch a fourth flush card. If you don't, you quickly give it up if your opponent bets into you.

Strong boards are often the key to whether to semi-bluff, bluff, or continue with a hand in heads-up play. The ultimate in personal judgment is always required in deciding how to the tournament, you should be able to read him rather well: his style, what's going through his mind, and so on. Remember that it takes far less strength to get involved in a pot heads-up than it does when even as few as three or four players are left.

"Raise and take it" will probably become the order of the day with the high upcard raising the smaller one. Suppose the low upcard is a deuce and you have a jack showing. You probably have a far greater chance of taking the pot with a raise than you would if the low card were an 8 and you held a 9. When you have nothing at all, you are better off just passing.

There are two occasions when you can limp in heads-up rather than raise. One is with a marginal hand such as a 9 up against an 8. If you have 7-10 in the hole, for example, you may want to take off a card. Although you are looking for that perfect 8, you might also catch one of your overcards and end up with the best pair. Another time you may want to flat-call with such a marginal hand is when you hold a three-flush and only your upcard is higher than your opponent's doorcard. You hope to either pair your high card or catch a fourth flush card. If you don't, you quickly give it up if your opponent bets into you.

Strong boards are often the key to whether to semi-bluff, bluff, or continue with a hand in heads-up play. The ultimate in personal judgment is always required in deciding how to best proceed with your hand in seven-card stud. ♠

Can I Make A Living Playing Low to Medium-Limit Poker?

That's one of the questions I am most frequently asked. My answer is a definite, "*Maybe.*" Actually, it *can* be done. I know a lot of people who are doing it. The question is, can *you* do it? (*Maybe.*) It isn't easy. It's a lot like having a job, except that you get to choose your own hours. But as a writer friend said, "Sure, you can choose your own hours, provided you choose every waking hour, seven days a week."

You should also be aware of a saying among medium and low-limit professional players: "It's a tough way to make an easy living."

Let's talk about making a living at these limits, and what you should consider before giving it a shot. By medium and lower limits, I mean limits of $10-$20 and under. A single person without a lot of expenses can make a living. A retired person can augment a pension and do quite well. But someone with a family, a mortgage, and two car payments had better be an exceptionally good player with great discipline.

If others are doing it, you can do it. But *how* do they do it? They are *very* good players who *really* know the game. They study. They have all the books. They've taken all the lessons. They think about poker as a business—seriously. As a professional you'll have to learn to pick your spots. You're looking for a game where people are just out to have a good time. They look like they can afford to lose some money.

You want to sit down in this game and make these people enjoy losing their money to you. That's right. You have to make them like it! That is the mark of a really good working player.

How do you make them like it? You sit in the game and become friendly with everyone. You talk to them and get them talking. You get them feeling good. And when you win a big pot, no one gets angry. They just laugh it off, and you laugh with them. And when they beat you out of a pot with a disastrous miracle draw, you laugh and say, "Nice hand. You really got me on that one."

It's very important that you do this because it makes people want to play with you. They won't mind losing their money to such a nice person. Just try being surly with them; let them get the idea that you're a poker hustler, and see how long they stay in your game.

Movement—playing in a game as long as it's a good game, and then moving on. Find those action games. Hit and run. Sure, it takes time and effort, but I never promised you strawberries in your champagne—or an easy time of it while you're trying to turn a living playing medium and low-limit poker. The only promise I'll make is this: The money you earn, *you will earn.*

The downside is that most of your opponents will be playing free and easy, not worried about money. But you will be playing for your living. You're giving up a psychological edge. This means that you need *strong* discipline. You cannot be casual about your play. You must play your best game *every session—every minute.*

If they have a bad day at work, most people still will get paid. If you have a bad day at work, you not only won't get paid, you'll have money taken from you!

This is not a profession for the faint of heart. But if you must do it (and don't do it unless your entire being cries out that you *must* do it), then forget about the ease and glamour. Go into it with your eyes open. Master it. Live it. Love it.

Before we go on, let's dream.

Dreams. Fantasies. Young boys dream about coming out of the bull pen in the bottom of the ninth with no one out, the basis loaded, a one-run lead—and striking out the next three batters to save the victory. Young girls fantasize about... I don't know; I've never been a young girl. And poker players imagine taking a pair of deuces in the pocket and making them stand up in the finals of the *World Series of Poker*. At last, the recognition due them as World Champion! *"And the crowd of admiring fans goes crazy."*

Reality says that more than 99.99 percent of us will never see this dream come true. Each year sees only one champion crowned out of the millions of poker players. And some people actually repeat as champions, making our chances of getting there even more infinitesimal.

John Fox said it for all of us in the title of his book, *Play Poker, Quit Work and Sleep Til Noon!* Now there's a dream we can all buy into. Some have succeeded in doing just that. Some have made it. Thousands try every year and go belly up.

Each day fresh talent arrives in cities that have a lot of public poker such as Las Vegas. They are brimming with hope and expectation. And every day the tired and beaten depart, disappearing as suddenly as they appeared, mostly with little notice taken of their coming or going.

But *some* do make it, and so the hopeful keep coming. And appearing. And disappearing. As a personal service to you, I have assessed *your* chances of success as a professional poker player. You have two chances: *slim* and *none*.

If that discourages you, you *should* be discouraged and give up all thought of being a poker pro. But if being shown your chances just makes you want it all the more—if the desire to be a professional poker player is equaled only by your desire to breathe—then go for it. That's the kind of desire it takes.

Desire. Commitment. Discipline. Courage. And somewhere along the way, you'll need poker skill. When you have all of that, you're still not ready. I have several questions for you to consider before you give up your job to become a full-time poker pro.

Do you have an adequate bankroll for the game you intend to play? I suggest that you have a rock-bottom minimum of 300-times the upper betting limit of your game as a playing bankroll. 400-times would be better. And I want to stress again that these are *rock-bottom minimums*.

Once you have established your bankroll, whatever its size, think of it as money to be used exclusively for playing poker.

If you find yourself having to extract living expenses from your bankroll, you are living too close to the edge. (There's more about this in Course Lesson 33, "The Fuel of Poker.")

Do you have enough money to cover your living expenses for six months? The competition could be tougher than you anticipate. It almost always is. You might get off to a slow start. If you have to begin living out of your bankroll, you'll find yourself under added pressure. You'll be playing with the rent money. That has been the downfall of many professional hopefuls.

Do you know what your living expenses are? If you've never thought seriously about it, I suggest that you do so now. You calculate them simply by first adding up your monthly expenses. Next, total the expenses you pay on a quarterly, semiannual, and annual basis. Divide by twelve to know what is required each month. Add these two figures together and there's the monthly nut you must overcome with your poker winnings.

It's at this point that a lot of potential pros see reality setting in and give up the whole idea. But if you still are determined to take your shot, or if you just want more to consider, let's pose some more questions for you to think about.

After taking the big step and becoming a poker pro, which of your expenses will increase? Which will decrease or be eliminated? Your drive to the poker room could be longer, or shorter, than the drive to your present job. Your wardrobe requirements might be entirely different.

What about the fringe benefits of your present job? Will you have to begin paying for your health insurance? What about your retirement plan? Figure all the perks that come your way now (at company expense) that you may need to replace. Company car? Expense account? Credit cards? Are you confident—*really confident*—that you can overcome all of this?

Do your present winnings indicate that by playing full-time, you'll do as well, or better than, you now do at your job?

Be completely honest with yourself.

Why are you thinking about making this move? Can you really do better? Or do you just like the idea of being a professional poker player? More honesty, please. Have you set reasonable win goals toward which you are willing to work? (Remember, this will be your profession, your *job*.) Do you have a wife, a husband, a family? Do they support you in this venture? If not, you're looking for trouble. Talk it over with them. Eliminate the stress going in. If you can't, you might have too much to overcome. How's your health? If you have problems, your new life-style might add stress instead of freedom.

Are you ready for the fact that your income might take some radical ups and downs? You might win $4,000 one month and only $400 the next month. Or it's even possible that you might have a *losing* month.

Can you leave your present job on good terms with your employer? It's mighty tempting to tell him to "shove it," but someday you might need that job again—or maybe a good reference.

Will your friends and neighbors understand that because you don't have a "regular" job, it doesn't mean that you have time to run their errands, watch their kids, or sit and chat endlessly?

How close do you now live to public poker rooms? Are there games nearby that you can rely on daily? Or will you have to move to Nevada or Southern California or some other area with plenty of public poker? This would be an additional expense. And keep in mind that where there are public poker rooms, you'll find people who have been playing every day, so you'll probably encounter a higher level of competition.

What about vacations? There will be a great temptation to play seven days a week, 365 days a year. That could lead to burnout. You'll still need vacations. That means time away from "work." No work, no pay. And there won't be any paid sick days either.

Do you have the discipline to maintain a schedule? Your time will be your own, and so will the motivation that keeps you moving toward your goal.

Ask yourself again about confidence. Can you really do it? Or is it just wishful thinking. Think about it. And then *think some more* before you decide. And here's a helpful tip: If this turns out to be a big decision for you to make, then you aren't ready to turn pro. You obviously aren't comfortable with making that move, for any number of reasons. The reasons don't matter; your comfort with the decision does. When you can make the decision with ease, *then* you'll be ready to go for it. Large luck! ♠

7 CARD STUD

The Final Word

To paraphrase an old one-liner, "There are only two people in the entire world of poker who are really willing to study the game—me and you—and I'm not too sure about you." My point here is: I want to become sure about you.

If you and I could walk in to a major cardroom and somehow stop the action for a moment and ask all those players, "How many of you are here to win money?" *Every* hand in the place would go up. We'd then have everyone resume playing as we strolled through the room observing.

It would soon become apparent that *the vast majority* did not come here to win money, or they wouldn't be playing so badly. Sure, they would like to win, but *mostly* they want to *play*. And they seem to be abiding by the old poker adage, "Next to playing and winning, is playing and losing. The important thing is playing."

Most poker players *do* have the will to win. What they *don't* have is the will to *prepare* to win.

By my estimation, only 15-to-20 percent of all poker players ever get a book on how win at the game. Notice that I used the word "get", not "study". Because I also estimate that 90 percent of those who do get a book of instruction won't study it. It's as if they believe that the act of buying the book and having it in their possession will give them the winning knowledge they need, maybe through the process of osmosis. They'll read through the book once, quickly, promise themselves to really study it later (some undetermined, unscheduled "later"), and then rush off to the poker game.

Most players just like the action. For many, the social process is the important thing. For a few—you and me—the idea is to leave the cardroom with more cash in our jeans than we came in with. Personally, I don't go to the poker room to play poker: I go to get the money.

I've given you the information you need to get the money, consistently. I have crammed twenty-five years of playing experience and study into this Course. But it won't be worth one blue farthing to you if it just lays around gathering dust.

So here's our plan. You've read through the Course. Now go back and read it again—just lightly, once over. At this point, the ideas will start to become familiar and will begin to be a part of your thinking—and your playing. *Now* you start *studying*.

Read a Lesson. Read it again. Think about it. Read it again. Now get away from it for a day. Then read it again. Next Lesson, repeat the process. When you've done this with all of the Lessons, set the Course aside for a couple of weeks and do it all over again. *Now* you've got it, and won't lose it. Then about every couple of months, take some time to lightly read through all the material again.

If you're beginning to think that this sounds like a lot of work—you're right! But nowhere in this Course have I promised you strawberries in your champagne, or an easy time in becoming a consistent winner. And I'll remind you of what

Easy Ed said about practicing: "When you are not practicing, someone, somewhere, *is* practicing. And when you meet him, he will beat you."

Many players, *right this instant*, are somewhere out there, studying poker. Some have taken my private Lessons. Many are studying this very Course you now hold. You had better get ready to meet them.

Here's my final "final word." It has also been my parting thought to my private students as I leave them at the end of the final session. Many thousands of poker players now have, or soon will have, this same information you've learned from this Course. Question: *"If they know what you know, how are you going to beat them?"*

Answer: *Discipline!*

Remember, it doesn't matter how good you *can* play, what matters is how good you *do* play. The player who holds his discipline and consciously works on eliminating mistakes, will be the consistent winner. Solid poker gets the money at the low and medium limits.

Forget about the will to win—instead, acquire the will to *prepare* to win.

Let me know how you do. ♠

Some Odds

Just to prove this Course isn't all sunshine, lollipops and roses, I have some numbers for you to memorize. Stop your moaning. Life can't be all fun all the time. Besides, knowing these numbers will make your life as a poker player easier.

You should know these drawing odds, at a minimum, without having to stop and think about them.

The Odds Against Making a Full House While You are Holding:

Three of a kind (3rd street) 2-to-1
Three of a kind and one other card (4th street) 2.5-to-1
Three of a kind and two other cards (5th street) 2.5-to-1
Three of a kind and three other cards (6th street) 4-to-1
Two pair (4th street) 3.5-to-1
Two pair and one other card (5th street) 5-to-1
Two pair and two other cards (6th street) 10-to-1

The Odds Against Making a Flush While You are Holding:

Three of a suit and one other card (4th street) 8.5-to-1
Three of a suit and two other cards (5th street) 23-to-1
Four of a suit (4th street) 1.25-to-1
Four of a suit and one other card (5th street) 1.75-to-1
Four of a suit and two other cards (6th street) 4.25-to-1

The Odds Against Making a Straight While You are Holding:

An open-end 3-straight and one other card 8-to-1
An open-end 3-straight and two other cards 22-to-1
An open-end 4-straight 1.5-to-1
An open-end 4-straight and one other card 2-to-1
An open-end 4-straight and two other cards 5-to-1
An inside 4-straight 3-to-1
An inside 4-straight and one other card 5-to-1
An inside 4-straight and two other cards 10-to-1

Recommended Reading

One of the questions my students most often ask me is, "What poker books do you think are worth reading?" I recommend just a few books that I believe are important reading for seven-card stud players.

To my way of thinking, the best poker book, whatever your game, is *Theory of Poker* by David Sklansky. It's not so much a strategy book as it is a "thinking" book. You'll learn to think about poker and devise your own strategies. It's the best thirty bucks of poker money you'll ever spend.

After you've mastered this Course and decide to move up in the limits to play $15-$30 seven-card stud and higher, I suggest that you read *Seven-Card Stud for Advanced Players* by David Sklansky, Mason Malmuth, and Ray Zee. Mike Caro has a piece of work titled *11 Days to 7-Stud Success*, which gives you daily "missions" to complete. Clear, concise information. Well worth the money.

Seven-Card Stud, The Waiting Game, by George Percy has long been a classic in the field. Although some of his strategies are now outdated, Percy's book is still very worthwhile.

Gary Oliver has written a dandy little book for low-limit players titled *Low-Limit Seven-Card Stud.* His section on practice hands is especially good.

Tournament players will find a wealth of information on their passion in Tom McEvoy's *Tournament Poker.* McEvoy has won more tournaments than anyone on the face of this planet, including the 1983 World Championship of Poker.

For an overview of the best ideas of the experts on tournament strategies, I recommend Shane Smith's book, *Poker Tournament Tips from the Pros.* Smith's "shortie" 32-pager titled *How to Win at Low-Limit Casino Poker* is a bargain.

Dana Smith, *Card Player* columnist and the editor of the book you are now reading, recommends two computer software programs on seven-card stud: *Turbo Seven-Card Stud* from Wilson Software, and ConJelCo's *Sozobon Poker for Windows* (which also includes a tournament mode). She believes that computer programs give you valuable practice away from casino and home games, so that you can make your strategy decisions in a less pressured environment.

Whether you want to play professionally, just play the game the best way the game can be played, or augment your income every month, I strongly suggest that you have these books and software in your poker library. ♠

THE CHAMPIONSHIP SERIES
POWERFUL BOOKS YOU MUST HAVE

CHAMPIONSHIP OMAHA (Omaha High-Low, Pot-limit Omaha, Limit High Omaha) by T. J. Cloutier & Tom McEvoy. Clearly-written strategies and powerful advice from Cloutier and McEvoy who have won four World Series of Poker titles in Omaha tournaments. Powerful advice shows you how to win at low-limit and high-stakes games, how to play against loose and tight opponents, and the differing strategies for rebuy and freezeout tournaments. Learn the best starting hands, when slowplaying a big hand is dangerous, what danglers are and why winners don't play them, why pot-limit Omaha is the only poker game where you sometimes fold the nuts on the flop and are correct in doing so and overall, how you can win a lot of money at Omaha! 230 pages, photos, illustrations, $39.95. Now only $29.95!

CHAMPIONSHIP STUD (Seven-Card Stud, Stud 8/or Better and Razz) by Dr. Max Stern, Linda Johnson, and Tom McEvoy. The authors, who have earned millions of dollars in major tournaments and cash games, eight World Series of Poker bracelets and hundreds of other titles in competition against the best players in the world show you the winning strategies for medium-limit side games as well as poker tournaments and a general tournament strategy that is applicable to any form of poker. Includes give-and-take conversations between the authors to give you more than one point of view on how to play poker. 200 pages, hand pictorials, photos. $29.95.

CHAMPIONSHIP HOLD'EM by T. J. Cloutier & Tom McEvoy. Hard-hitting hold'em the way it's played today in both limit cash games and tournaments. Get killer advice on how to win more money in rammin'-jammin' games, kill-pot, jackpot, shorthanded, and other types of cash games. You'll learn the thinking process before the flop, on the flop, on the turn, and at the river with specific suggestions for what to do when good or bad things happen plus 20 illustrated hands with play-by-play analyses. Specific advice for rocks in tight games, weaklings in loose games, experts in solid games, how hand values change in jackpot games, when you should fold, check, raise, reraise, check-raise, slowplay, bluff, and tournament strategies for small buy-in, big buy-in, rebuy, incremental add-on, satellite and big-field major tournaments. Wow! Easy-to-read and conversational, if you want to become a lifelong winner at limit hold'em, you need this book! 320 Pages, Illustrated, Photos. $39.95. Now only $29.95!

CHAMPIONSHIP NO-LIMIT & POT-LIMIT HOLD'EM by T. J. Cloutier & Tom McEvoy New Cardoza Edition! The definitive guide to winning at two of the world's most exciting poker games! Written by eight time World Champion players T. J. Cloutier (1998 and 2002 Player of the Year) and Tom McEvoy (the foremost author on tournament strategy) who have won millions of dollars each playing no-limit and pot-limit hold'em in cash games and major tournaments around the world. You'll get all the answers here - no holds barred - to your most important questions: How do you get inside your opponents' heads and learn how to beat them at their own game? How can you tell how much to bet, raise, and reraise in no-limit hold'em? When can you bluff? How do you set up your opponents in pot-limit hold'em so that you can win a monster pot? What are the best strategies for winning no-limit and pot-limit tournaments, satellites, and supersatellites? You get rock-solid and inspired advice from two of the most recognizable figures in poker — advice that you can bank on. If you want to become a winning player, a champion, you must have this book. 288 pages, paperback, illustrations, photos. $29.95

THE CHAMPIONSHIP SERIES
POWERFUL BOOKS YOU MUST HAVE

CHAMPIONSHIP TOURNAMENT POKER by Tom McEvoy. New Cardoza Edition! Rated by pros as best book on tournaments ever written and enthusiastically endorsed by more than 5 world champions, this is the definitive guide to winning tournaments and a must for every player's library. McEvoy lets you in on the secrets he has used to win millions of dollars in tournaments and the insights he has learned competing against the best players in the world. Packed solid with winning strategies for all 11 games in the World Series of Poker, with extensive discussions of 7-card stud, limit hold'em, pot and no-limit hold'em, Omaha high-low, re-buy, half-half tournaments, satellites, strategies for each stage of tournaments. Tons of essential concepts and specific strategies jam-pack the book. Phil Hellmuth, 1989 WSOP champion says, [this] is the world's most definitive guide to winning poker tournaments. 416 pages, paperback, $29.95.

CHAMPIONSHIP TABLE (at the World Series of Poker) by Dana Smith, Ralph Wheeler, and Tom McEvoy. New Cardoza Edition! From 1970 when the champion was presented a silver cup, to the present when the champion was awarded more than $2 million, Championship Table celebrates three decades of poker greats who have competed to win poker's most coveted title. This book gives you the names and photographs of all the players who made the final table, pictures the last hand the champion played against the runner-up, how they played their cards, and how much they won. This book also features fascinating interviews and conversations with the champions and runners-up and interesting highlights from each Series. This is a fascinating and invaluable resource book for WSOP and gaming buffs. In some cases the champion himself wrote "how it happened," as did two-time champion Doyle Brunson when Stu Ungar caught a wheel in 1980 on the turn to deprive "Texas Dolly" of his third title. Includes tons of vintage photographs. 208 pages, paperback, $19.95.

CHAMPIONSHIP SATELLITE STRATEGY by Brad Dougherty & Tom McEvoy. In 2002 and 2003 satellite players won their way into the $10,000 WSOP buy-in and emerged as champions, winning more than $2 million each. You can too! You'll learn specific, proven strategies for winning almost any satellite. Learn the 10 ways to win a seat at the WSOP and other big tournaments, how to win limit hold'em and no-limit hold'em satellites, one-table satellites for big tournaments, and online satellites, plus how to play the final table of super satellites. McEvoy and Daugherty sincerely believe that if you practice these strategies, you can win your way into any tournament for a fraction of the buy-in. You'll learn how much to bet, how hard to pressure opponents, how to tell when an opponent is bluffing, how to play deceptively, and how to use your chips as weapons of destruction. Includes a special chapter on no-limit hold'em satellites! 256 pages. illustrated hands, photos, glossary. $24.95.

CHAMPIONSHIP PRACTICE HANDS by T. J. Cloutier & Tom McEvoy. Two tournament legends show you how to become a winning tournament player. Get inside their heads as they think they way through the correct strategy at 57 limit and no-limit practice hands. Cloutier & McEvoy show you how to use your skill and intuition to play strategic hands for maximum profit in real tournament scenarios and how 45 key hands were played by champions in turnaround situations at the WSOP. By sharing their analysis on how the winners and losers played key hands, you'll gain tremendous insights into how tournament poker is played at the highest levels. Learn how champions think and how they play major hands in strategic tournament situations, Cloutier and McEvoy believe that you will be able to win your share of the profits in today's tournaments -- and join them at the championship table far sooner than you ever imagined. 288 pages, illustrated with card pictures, $29.95

DOYLE BRUNSON'S SUPER SYSTEM
A COURSE IN POKER POWER!
by World Champion Doyle Brunson

CONSIDERED BY PROS THE BEST POKER BOOK EVER WRITTEN
This is the **classic** book on every major no-limit game played today and is considered by the pros to be one of the **best books ever written** on poker! **Jam-packed** with **advanced strategies**, theories, tactics and money-making techniques—no serious poker player can afford to be without this **essential** book! Hardbound, and packed with 624 pages of hard-hitting information, this is truly a **must-buy** for aspiring pros. Includes 50 pages of the most precise poker statistics ever published!

CHAPTERS WRITTEN BY GAME'S SUPERSTARS
The best theorists and poker players in the world, Dave Sklansky, Mike Caro, Chip Reese, Bobby Baldwin and Doyle Brunson, a book by champions for aspiring pros—cover the **essential** strategies and **advanced play** in their respective specialties. Three world champions and two master theorists and players provide non-nonsense winning advice on making money at the tables.

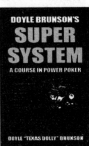

LEARN WINNING STRATEGIES FOR THE MAJOR POKER GAMES
The important money games today are covered in depth by these **poker superstars**. You'll learn seven-card stud, draw poker, lowball, seven-card low stud (razz), high-low split (cards speak) and high-low declare; and the most popular game in the country today, hold'em (limit and no-limit). Each game is covered in detail with the **important winning concepts** and strategies clearly explained so that anyone can become a **bigger money** winner.

SERIOUS POKER PLAYERS MUST HAVE THIS BOOK
This is **mandatory reading** for aspiring poker pros, players planning to enter tournaments, players ready to play no-limit. Doyle Brunson's Super System is also ideal for average players seeking to move to higher stakes games for bigger wins and more challenges.

To order, send $29.95 by check or money order to Cardoza Publishing

POWERFUL POKER SIMULATIONS
A MUST FOR SERIOUS PLAYERS WITH A COMPUTER!
IBM compatibles CD ROM Win 95, 98, 2000, NT, ME, XP - Full Color Graphics

Play interactive poker against these **incredible** full color poker simulation programs—they're the absolute **best** method to improve your game. Computer players act like real players. All games let you set the limits and rake, have fully programmable players, adjustable lineup, stat tracking, and Hand Analyzer for starting hands. Mike Caro, the world's foremost poker theoretician says, "Amazing...a steal for under $500...get it, it's great." Includes free telephone support. **New Feature!** - "Smart Advisor" gives expert advice for every play in every game!

NEW!
Windows Versions
More Features!

1. TURBO TEXAS HOLD'EM FOR WINDOWS - $89.95 - Choose which players, how many, 2-10, you want to play, create loose/tight game, control check-raising, bluffing, position, sensitivity to pot odds, more! Also, instant replay, pop-up odds, Professional Advisor, keeps track of play statistics. Free bonus: Hold'em Hand Analyzer analyzes all 169 pocket hands in detail, their win rates under any conditions you set. Caro says this "hold'em software is the most powerful ever created." Great product!

2. TURBO SEVEN-CARD STUD FOR WINDOWS - $89.95 - Create any conditions of play; choose number of players (2-8), bet amounts, fixed or spread limit, bring-in method, tight/loose conditions, position, reaction to board, number of dead cards, stack deck to create special conditions, instant replay. Terrific stat reporting includes analysis of starting cards, 3-D bar charts, graphs. Play interactively, run high speed simulation to test strategies. Hand Analyzer analyzes starting hands in detail. Wow!

3. TURBO OMAHA HIGH-LOW SPLIT FOR WINDOWS - $89.95 -Specify any playing conditions; betting limits, number of raises, blind structures, button position, aggressiveness/ passiveness of opponents, number of players (2-10), types of hands dealt, blinds, position, board reaction, specify flop, turn, river cards! Choose opponents, use provided point count or create your own. Statistical reporting, instant replay, pop-up odds, high speed simulation to test strategies, amazing Hand Analyzer, much more!

4. TURBO OMAHA HIGH FOR WINDOWS - $89.95 - Same features as above, but tailored for the Omaha High-only game. Caro says program is "an electrifying research tool...it can clearly be worth thousands of dollars to any serious player. A must for Omaha High players.

5. TURBO 7 STUD 8 OR BETTER - $89.95 - Brand new with all the features you expect from the Wilson Turbo products: the latest artificial intelligence, instant advice and exact odds, play versus 2-7 opponents, enhanced data charts that can be exported or printed, the ability to fold out of turn and immediately go to the next hand, ability to peek at opponents hand, optional warning mode that warns you if a play disagrees with the advisor, and automatic testing mode that can run up to 50 tests unattended. Challenge tough computer players who vary their styles for a truly great poker game.

6. TOURNAMENT TEXAS HOLD'EM - $59.95
Set-up for tournament practice and play, this realistic simulation pits you against celebrity look-alikes. Tons of options let you control tournament size with 10 to 300 entrants, select limits, ante, rake, blind structures, freezeouts, number of rebuys and competition level of opponents - average, tough, or toughest. Pop-up status report shows how you're doing vs. the competition. Save tournaments in progress to play again later. Additional feature allows you to quickly finish a folded hand and go on to the next.